SPORTSMAN'S LEGACY

BOOKS BY
WILLIAM G. TAPPLY

THE BRADY COYNE NOVELS

NON-FICTION

SPORTSMAN'S LEGACY

WILLIAM G. TAPPLY

LYONS & BURFORD, PUBLISHERS

Lyons & Burford
31 West 21 Street
New York, NY 10010.

PRINTED IN THE UNITED STATES OF AMERICA

Design by Lynne Amft Design

10 9 8 7 6 5 4 3 2 1

Library of Congress Cataloging-in-Publication Data
Tapply, William G.
    Sportsman's legacy / William G. Tapply.
        p.   cm.
    ISBN 1-55821-244-2
    1. Tapply, William G.   2. Hunting stories.   3. Fishing stories.
    4. Sportswriters — United States — Biography.   5. Fathers and sons.
    6. Tapply, H.G. Horace G.), 1910-   . I. Title.
    SK17.T29A3 1993
    799'.092 — dc20
        [B]   93-8884
                                                                          CIP

Dedicated with love, admiration, and appreciation to Muriel Tapply, my mother, the other (and Dad would say the better) half of this equation and a skilled sportswoman in her own right, who believes that fathers and sons should fish and hunt together as often as possible, and who makes the world's best applesauce cake, and who had the uncommon wisdom to pick out the right father for me.

CONTENTS

AUTHOR'S NOTE

I am grateful to Nick Lyons for encouraging me to tackle this project. It has been, more than any other in my life, a genuine labor of love.

The incidents and people of this memoir are as accurately recalled as my memory allows. I have, without telling them why, checked my recollections against those of my parents. Mum remembers things sharply, and I depend on her for the truth. Dad admits that his memory sometimes fails him, and he cheerfully practices the novelist's art of "improving" on history if he thinks it will make a better story.

I don't think this history needs improving, and I've tried not to do it. But insofar as I have, I am confident that I have remained faithful to the important truths.

I appreciate Mum and Dad's forbearance and innocent collaboration. They patiently answered my oblique inquiries and debated the details of stories from our shared past, and they intuitively understood that I did not want them questioning my sudden interest.

During one of these nostalgic encounters, Dad looked at Mum and said, "Someone must've asked him to write my obituary."

She rolled her eyes. "Oh, for heaven's sake," she said.

—W.G.T.
ACTON, MASSACHUSETTS
APRIL 1993

INTRODUCTION

$\mathcal{I}$ was sitting beside a Rocky Mountain stream last fall watching a rainbow trout sip midges off the surface and wondering how I might catch him when a stranger wandered up the path, stopped beside me, and squinted at the water. "Nice fish," he said. "You gonna try for him?"

I told him I intended to eventually, but for now I was content to watch him.

"Mind if I watch with you?"

I patted the grass beside me. "Pull up a seat."

He was about my age, I guessed, and it quickly became evident that he shared my appreciation for trout-hunting as a spectator sport. We talked about bugs and fish, mountains and rivers, and in the course of our conversation we exchanged names and shook hands properly. He told me he had retired early from the computer business so that he could attend to more important things like fishing. I told him I wrote for a living, sometimes about fishing, which was almost as good as being retired.

He smacked his palm with his fist. "Tapply!" he said. "Of course. I love your stuff."

I smiled modestly.

"This is great," he said. "Listen, when I was a kid I used to clip your columns out of *Field & Stream* every month. I kept 'em in a scrapbook. Hell, you're my hero."

"When you were a kid," I said, "I suspect I was a kid, too. That was my father who wrote the column."

He frowned. "You're not Tap? You don't write Tap's Tips?"

"That's my Dad."

"Aw, I'm sorry."

"Don't be," I said. "Happens all the time. He's my hero, too."

———

Enough potboilers are published every year to convince me that many talented and idolized people make perfectly frightening parents, and that their offspring's published revelations make best-selling books.

This book will shock and amaze you: H.G. Tapply really *could* tie flies and paddle a canoe and catch fish. But the thing he did best of all was raise a son. He's still doing all those things, and he continues to do them with rare excellence.

This book will boil no pots.

———

I'm not sure where in my anatomy the hunting impulse resides — in my genes, some would say, or in my soul — but it's certainly there as, I'm convinced, it is in all of us. The human species would not have adapted and survived if we couldn't hunt. Those who lacked the instinct for it simply did not pass along their genes. Hunting and gathering constituted the primary occupation of the human male for all but the most recent eyeblink of human evolution. Such powerful adaptive mechanisms do not disappear easily.

Hunting, of course, includes fishing. It's all the same — that easy retreat into a predatory mode that feels too natural not to be genetically given. Whether I'm following a bird dog through grouse cover or creeping along the banks of a trout stream, I know I'm hunting. I hear and smell and see everything most acutely at these times. I am a fully alive and functioning human as I otherwise rarely am. I can easily imagine hunting for survival. Indeed, the survival of my sanity often seems to depend on it.

There is still that triumphant feeling that a successful hunt produces — a fish is landed, a bird is shot. My ancestors, I'm sure, exulted when they slew a mammoth, and they were tribal heroes when they dragged home an edible trophy. But the more I hunt and fish, the less relevant the trophy becomes. I don't need to shoot birds or catch fish to fulfill my powerful predatory impulses. I put back most of the fish I catch, and I feel little loss when I fail to land one. It no longer bothers me when I shoot and miss, as I usually do.

Seducing a trout into striking my fly and getting a fair shot at a flying grouse convince me I'm an excellent predator, and I am fulfilled.

Today an increasing number of people are denying this most basic aspect of the human character. They call hunting "primitive," which it surely is, but which surely doesn't make it immoral, as they contend. Or they call it "cruel," which it needn't be, or "sadistic," which it is only in its perversions. They sublimate the hunter-gatherer in themselves by playing tennis or the stock market — or by vilifying hunters and fishermen.

Most folks who haven't experienced our "blood sports" remain neutral on the subject, and that's fine. Others, however, become downright self-righteous and judgmental, and that frightens me. I worry about which side the neutrals will eventually come down on.

I'm glad so many people prefer concrete and air conditioning and their own perversions of the hunting urge, for there are already too many people crowding our rivers and woods. But I feel sorry for them, too. They have the same legacy that I do. Their ancestors gave them hunting, but they have not acknowledged the gift.

So I'm completely convinced that I was born with the urge to slip into nature and to try to creep up on wild things, and when I do it, I feel as wild and as natural as they are. This is my legacy. Dad did not give these instincts to me.

But he nurtured them. He gave me the outdoors, and mostly by bringing me along with him and allowing me to absorb it in my own way at my own pace, he taught me how to enjoy it fully.

He had no interest in cloning himself. Nor did he hope to create a fly-casting wing-shooting prodigy— which is just as well, because I surely would have disappointed him with my modest skills. He kept it simple and allowed it to be natural and fun. If Dad had any ulterior motive, it was to cultivate an amiable sporting companion. In that regard, he did everything right. We have always liked each other.

But he was no weekend parent. He did not limit his attentions to our times outdoors. Fatherhood was full-time work for Dad. When I was about ten, I took up the clarinet. Instead of buying me a metronome and sending me off to a soundproof room to squeak my way through my scales, he sat with me and beat time against the arm of his chair with his pipe. My childhood goal was to play shortstop for the Red Sox (Don Buddin, the incumbent during those impressionable years of mine, was fallible enough to make my dream seem realistic). So Dad threw me ten thousand grounders in the backyard, and on every one he yelled, "*Charge* the ball. Watch it all the way into your glove." When I took up archery, Dad bought himself a bow and asked me to show him how to shoot. Then my mother and Martha, my sister, tried it, liked it, and were good at it. We joined a field archery club. The four of us traveled all over New England to shoot in weekend tournaments. Martha and Mum won trophies regularly. There was no shame in doing things as a family in those days. When I decided to try out for the basketball team, Dad built a backboard, nailed it to the oak tree out back, and retrieved missed shots for me. When I made the team, he skipped out of work early to join my mother in dingy junior high school gyms and watch my afternoon games.

He moved his family into the country, and endured the long daily commute into the city without complaint, so that I could grow up with woods and fields and a pond out back.

He respected my judgment, even when I was young. He allowed me to make my own choices knowing, I'm certain, that I'd make plenty of bad ones, but trusting that I would learn from them, which is generally how it worked out. I can recall his ordering me to do only two things in my life — study Latin and learn to type — choices I surely would not have made on my own and which I am grateful he forced on me. Otherwise, he let me figure out things for myself, such as when the lawn needed mowing.

———••———

A friend of mine recently lost his father to cancer. "I sat with my Dad for his last twenty-four hours," he told me, "and I was finally able to say the things that I hadn't said to him in all my life. It was the hardest thing I've ever done."

Dad and I never run out of things to talk about, but I am content that he and I have said everything that needs saying already. It's never been hard.

Anyway, what I have to say wouldn't take long. "Thanks, Pop," would do it.

CHAPTER ONE

LAST HUNT

*O*n a crisp New Hampshire morning two years ago last October, Skip Rood and I pulled into the peastone driveway on Pond Road in Alton. Mum and Dad were expecting us for coffee before we began our day's hunt. "Let's see if we can talk Tap into joining us," said Skip.

I shook my head. "He won't come. He doesn't hunt anymore."

"I'll convince him."

"He's pretty stubborn. Says he's too old. Arthritis, bad back, stiff neck, cranky knee, hernia. He doesn't complain, but those are his facts. I've tried. He says his hunting days are over."

"He'll come."

"Bet a buck he won't."

"You're on."

I felt pretty smug. It was a sure bet.

The last time I had hunted with Dad had been more than a decade earlier. Birds were scarce in our old New Hampshire covers that day, and Bucky, Dad's aging Brittany, ran wild and bumped the few that were there out of range. Sometime in the afternoon we were skirting the edges of a little boggy tongue of alder when a woodcock jumped at Dad's feet. I can still see it clearly—the "little russet fellow," as our old friend Burt Spiller called them, twittering and struggling to the alder tops, pausing there in perfect silhouette against the sky directly in front of Dad, his gun rising instinctively to his shoulder.

I mentally recited an epitaph to that doomed bird. Dad was a deadly wingshot, especially on woodcock.

"Bang-bang," he said, conversationally.

He did not pull the trigger. The woodcock flew away.

Back in the car, I said, "What the hell was that all about?"

He feigned confusion. "Huh?"

"Saying 'bang-bang.' Not shooting."

"Safety stuck."

"Sure."

He grinned. "Don't buy that one, huh?"

"Nope."

He gazed out the car window. "Guess I don't have the heart for it anymore. I've shot an awful lot of birds. I *do* love 'em, you know." He shrugged. "Anyway, I *did* shoot that one. In my head. I just decided to put him back, like a trout."

That's when I knew that Dad's hunting days were over.

We sat around the table in the sun-drenched kitchen nook and watched the chickadees and finches compete with the squirrels at Dad's elaborate birdfeeder outside. Waldo, Skip's Brittany, lay under our feet. Dad dangled his hand to scratch the dog's ears. Mum poured coffee.

"I don't know how many covers old Waldo's got left in him," said Skip mournfully. "He's slowing down, getting old." He shook his head. "Best damned grouse dog I ever saw, too."

"Better than Seegars?" said Dad.

Seegars had been Waldo's sire. Dad had hunted with Skip and Seegars one dog generation earlier.

"Waldo's the best," said Skip matter-of-factly. "Everyone who hunts with him calls him Waldo the Wonder Dog. Never saw a dog that would point grouse the way Waldo does."

"Seegars was awfully good," mused Dad.

"You ain't seen nothin' til you've seen Waldo." Skip shrugged, then said, "Why don't you come with us, watch him work?"

"I'd love to," said Dad.

Skip caught my eye and grinned.

Dad put on one of the several blaze-red corduroy hunting shirts that Mum had made for him over the years. All its trips through the washer had faded it to pink. Then the four of us piled into Skip's wagon — Dad and Skip up front, Waldo and I in back.

It felt familiar. I had spent a lot of time in back seats with bird dogs as a kid. I understood that as long as I could demonstrate my mastery of the principle that children should be seen and not heard, I would be allowed to go along with the men. So while Dad and Burt Spiller or Harold Blaisdell or Lee Wulff or any of the others he fished and hunted with debated politics or economics or dog training or fly patterns up front, I sat in back with the dog, and both of us practiced the art of being seen and not heard.

I learned a lot that way. It's not a bad skill for an adult to cultivate, either, I've since decided.

Skip drove to one of our favorite old covers. Dad and I had discovered this classic grouse and woodcock hotspot one autumn afternoon twenty-five or thirty years earlier when a great horned owl flew across the dirt road in front of the car. "That," Dad said as he braked to a stop, "is a sign."

My father is a rationalist. He doesn't believe in portents, or superstitions, or even God. So I laughed. "What do you mean, a sign?"

"The owl is a predator," he said. "So I ask you. What's he preying on?"

"Chipmunks, probably," I shrugged.

"True. But did you see the alders and those old apple trees in there? There's fruit on those trees. It looks awful birdy. Let's have us a little ex-plore."

The owl, of course, had nothing to do with it.

An old woodsroad ended at a barway a hundred feet into the woods. On the right-hand side of the road, young hardwood sloped down to a brook where Baldwin apples mingled with hemlock and alder, and Dad and I found a brood of grouse among them on that day of discovery. We chased a single up to the crown of the hill where a stand of birch whips held a flight of woodcock.

I don't recall how many birds we took out of there that day. Probably not many. Duke, our setter, tended to get excited by too much birdscent and bust them wild, and I was not — still am not — a very good wingshot. Dad always chose the thickest routes where shooting was most difficult. He claimed that that's where the dog should be, and it was his dog, and the master should hunt with the dog. I know for a fact, however, that he always tried to arrange for his partner to get the good shots, even when such an advantage was wasted on me.

Back in the car that afternoon, Dad spread our topographic map on his knees, traced the lines with his forefinger, then drew a circle on it with a black felt-tip pen and printed the legend: "The Owl Cover."

I hadn't visited the Owl Cover for a decade — since Dad quit hunting — before that morning with Skip and Waldo.

Skip nosed the wagon up the woodsroad and stopped at the barway. "Looks different," said Dad, peering out the window. The oaks that had been saplings the day the owl flew across the road had grown to tall mature trees. The gnarled old Baldwins were bare of fruit. "The cover's past its prime," he said. He turned to scratch Waldo's ears. "Kinda gray of muzzle and slow of foot. Happens to the best of us."

"I bet it still holds birds," said Skip.

We climbed out of the wagon. Skip and I uncased our shotguns. "Where's your gun?" said Skip to Dad.

"Didn't bring one," he said. "I can hunt without a gun. I'll follow Bill around. I just want to see Waldo work."

I arched my eyebrows at Skip, who refused to meet my glance.

We angled down the slope toward the brook, with Skip on my right and Waldo zig-zagging between us. Dad followed along behind me. I tried to pick easy routes so he wouldn't lag too far behind. After a few minutes he said to me, "Hey! Hunt, will you? Don't pussy-foot around on my account. I can still keep up with the likes of you."

Waldo criss-crossed in front of us, working perfectly, and

near the brook he locked into a point. "Woodcock," announced Skip. "His grouse points are different."

I stood at ready while Skip moved in. He kicked out the woodcock. It corkscrewed up between us. I shot and missed. Skip fired and the little bird toppled. "Fetch," said Skip, and Waldo brought the bird to him.

"Tough shot," said Dad from behind me. "He made a right-angle turn just as you touched off."

"Thanks," I said. "I wasn't going to mention it." Dad had always helped me with my excuses. I'd hunted with him for a long time before I began to notice that he didn't make excuses for himself.

We found no more birds in the Owl Cover that morning. It had grown elderly and no longer looked very birdy. Back in Skip's wagon Dad said, "Thanks, men. I enjoyed it. Waldo's something, all right. You better drop me off now, so you can get serious."

"Oh, come along," said Skip. "We've got some good covers to hit. Besides, you haven't seen Waldo on a grouse yet."

"Nope. That was enough."

Skip shrugged. He knew as well as I did that it was no use to argue with Tap.

As we drove back to Pond Road, Dad turned to me from the front seat and said, "Did that remind you of anything?"

"What, me missing a woodcock? That conjured up a thousand identical memories, all equally embarrassing."

"Not that. I mean me tagging along behind you. Remember?"

I nodded. "Sure do. That was a while ago, huh?"

He smiled. "I was younger then than you are now."

I hunted with Dad for two years before I took my first shot at a flying grouse or woodcock. Just about every autumn weekend I trailed behind him through the thickest, muckiest terrain in New Hampshire, following, literally, in his footsteps, as I would metaphorically through much of my life. I did not carry a gun. I watched and learned, and while he did all the shooting, I *did* hunt.

So on that morning three Octobers ago when Dad followed me, gunless, through the Owl Cover, we both understood that a circle had been closed. I think he enjoyed the inevitable symmetry of it, although it saddened me.

That afternoon on the way back to Boston, Skip demanded his buck. I protested. "You used Waldo for a lure. Not fair. You know how he loves good dog work."

"That wasn't the only reason he came and you know it."

I nodded. "Okay," I said. "Conceded. But he didn't hunt."

"You mean he didn't carry a gun," said Skip. "There's a difference. You know that, too."

I forked over a dollar.

For the past two seasons Dad has stoutly declined Skip's invitations. "This'll be Waldo's last season for sure," Skip always says. "But you oughta see him. He's better than ever."

Dad waves his hand. "You boys go ahead, have fun."

We do have fun. I've been lucky enough to form hunting and fishing partnerships with some good men through the years. But for me it's never quite the same without Dad.

CHAPTER TWO

1 9 1 8

"*H*ey," Dad liked to say whenever a small mishap or minor setback befell me, "life is stern and earnest." He usually smiled when he recited this little homily, and I understood it was his way of reminding me to put things into perspective. Busting off a big trout or missing an easy straightaway shot at a grouse could seem monumentally tragic to a boy.

I didn't buy that "stern and earnest" stuff, of course. Life — or mine, at least — was easy and carefree. It was, I figured, just Dad's gentle way of mocking my impatience with my own fallibility. Eventually I came to realize that he meant it quite sincerely.

Dad's legacy, of course, is mine, too.

I have in my possession the diary that George Samuel Tapply kept during his second and third crossings of the North Atlantic in 1918. I don't know if he kept a diary of his first crossing. The record of his fourth trip is forever lost. The only other remembrance of Dad's father — my Grampie — is an intricately inlaid wooden cribbage board he made. Dad and I still peg out our games on it. I covet it.

When the United States entered the Great War, George Tapply left his wife and seven-year-old son, Horace, to re-enlist in the Navy as chief quartermaster on the *Ticonderoga*, a transport ship that carried troops to the battlefields of France. Dad does not talk much about those years. I do know that sometime after his father went to sea, his mother sent him to live with relatives in Wells, Maine, while she remained in Waltham to nurse victims of the influenza epidemic.

Meanwhile, George was at war. In May of 1918, while anchored in a French harbor, he wrote, "I am somewhat homesick today and have been thinking lots about my dear little wife and the cutest and dearest little boy in the world, Horace my little boy. It is awful to get so blue but when I think of the many others who are over here and do not get home at all till the war is over, I think I am not so bad off. Another ship was torpedoed just outside this port last night. The subs are very busy lately."

A few days later: "I have been very homesick today, and wrote a letter to my wife and as it had to be passed by the censoring officer I could not tell or say numerous things I should have under other circumstances. I do not like the idea of any one reading my letters to my wife because I am so lonely and homesick and feel like writing a loving letter and don't want them to read it. I wrote a poem to my wife last night, in bed, about eleven o'clock. Was just thinking of how I should have loved to be home with her and to relieve her mind. I wrote the poem which I called 'Longing for You.' "

By mid-June, the *Ticonderoga* was headed back to America to pick up another shipload of troops. "Have seen no subs yet," wrote Chief Quartermaster Tapply, "but may before morning, as they may be following us along and close in at nightfall, a habit of theirs. It is going to be a case of 'expecting' all of the way over this trip, because it is known there are large German submarines between here and America, some of those large ones 500 feet long and capable of 14 or 15 knots with large guns. I had just as soon meet one, but would like to be within a few hundred miles of shore."

June 20: "Received another warning today of submarines off the coast. I guess my dear little wife is some nervous, as she probably knows I am on my way back by now. Will be very glad to get in so I can get to see her. I miss her more and more every day, and live in hope that when the war is over to be alive and well. The chances are great for getting hit while running the blockade, but I figure my chances good if we get a chance to launch the boats. The excitement is worthwhile, though, and I shall have lots to think about when it is all over."

Two days later he wrote, "We lost a man, or boy, seventeen years old, overboard last night in a terrible storm, which raged all night. The poor fellow must have had a terrible feeling to be out in that rough sea and see the ship go along with no hope of getting picked up. No one saw him go over, but he was missed at 12:30. He came off watch at midnight. A search was made but could not find him. This morning some of the fellows said they thought they heard a cry of 'man overboard,' but as the wind was so strong it was very indistinct. Poor fellow. He could not last long in a sea like that. Oh, it was a terrible night out. The wind was blowing a hurricane and I don't think it ever rained harder, and the ship rolling terrible, with a 60-mile gale blowing. We all feel bad for him and his folks. I wish the war would hurry up and get over, for things like that kind of give one the feeling that he does not want to go to sea anymore."

They made harbor on June 25. By mid-July the *Ticonderoga* had begun its third crossing. "I do not feel very well today," George wrote on July 13. "My stomach is on the blink, probably I have eaten too much watermelon, as they are very cheap in Norfolk and the commissary steward bought quite a lot and brought them along. I hope I shall feel better after today. If I was home just now I would as soon be sick a few days, because I would have my wife to take care of me. ... The Capt. made an inspection of the ship this A.M. and gave me quite a compliment on the room. We finished painting it the day before yesterday, and it did look good. I guess when he looked up at my bunk and saw my wife's picture with Horace on one side of her and me on the other, he couldn't say much else. ... This trip has a funny feeling to it and I can not but feel that something is going to happen. For the last week all kinds of precautions have been taken, and all the life boats have been thoroughly overhauled and everybody must take a life belt with them if they leave their quarters."

July 24: "The ocean escort U.S.S. *Galveston* turned back today, so we have no protection except our own guns. It is very dangerous waters through which we will be going till we strike port — probably next Sunday if we do not get sunk. It is very hard to see a sub at night and I expect we will lose one or more ships tonight, as we know there are submarines around us."

July 26: "Things started last night at 7:30 P.M. when we heard an explosion and saw the ship right abeam of us, and only four hundred yards away, the U.S.S. *Tippicanoe*, get torpedoed and start to sink. In five minutes she had three boats in the water. ... Somehow this trip seems kind of funny to me, and I have had a very queer feeling about it, and although we expect to arrive in port Sunday we have two more nights to put in yet, and something more is apt to happen, for we know that the subs are following us and tonight they will close in and some poor ship is going to take the deep six."

By August 22, the *Ticonderoga* had delivered its troops and turned back for the States. "Warnings are coming in quite often, and there are lots of subs out operating, but we will hope they do not happen to see us. This is like a game of hide and go seek, only if you are seen you go down."

August 28: "Our pleasure trip was rudely interrupted at sundown when a submarine came up on our port side and about three miles away ... We opened up with our three-inch and then the sub went under. A few minutes after we saw the wake of a torpedo coming right towards us from the starboard side about 25 miles an hour and just by sheer luck missed us by only a few feet or went under the stern, I could not make out which."

On September 5 the *Ticonderoga* had safely made port. "I heard today no one was to be granted leave, but I am going to see the First Lt. and see if mine can be granted. I am so blue now I do not know how I would feel if I had to go across again and not see my wife and boy."

I don't know if he was granted his leave and made it home for his son's eighth birthday on September 18, but a couple of weeks later the *Ticonderoga* once again weighed anchor. I assume Chief Quartermaster Tapply kept a diary, but I have only a scrapbook of newspaper clippings for an account of his fourth crossing. One of the faded yellow clippings reprints the letter that George Tapply wrote to his mother on October 10, 1918, from aboard the British ship, R.M.S. *Grampian*.

"Dear Mother: I thank God I am here and alive to write to you. As you can see by the writing paper, I am on board one of your own country's Royal Mail ships, now doing convoy duty and carrying American troops across the pond. I am bound for New York.

"I have no doubt you will see in the papers of our disaster, but not knowing what might be put in and whether the names of the twenty-eight survivors will be published, I thought I would drop you a few lines as soon as possible and relieve your mind from worry. I am all right but slightly wounded in the left leg just above the ankle by shrapnel and may have to go to the hospital for a few days before I can come home to see you. The wound is not very bad, but as it was five days without any medical attention, it is somewhat sore and inflamed, but it ought to enable me to come home in a week or so.

"It is God's will that my time has not yet arrived for me to die, for I faced death and came through alive, while 220 other men did not.

"It was on the morning of Sept. 30 in the middle Atlantic at daybreak, we were attacked by a submarine which opened up on us without any warning and the first two shots carried away our bridge, setting it on fire and killing five men who were on it. The Captain was very badly wounded, having a shrapnel cut away some of the bone at the knee and his face and head all cut up. When I came forward he was crawling off the bridge and I helped to carry him aft, away from the fire, as the bridge by that time was a roaring furnace. The three-inch forward gun had a chance to fire only one shot when a shell hit it and killed the entire crew. The sub then came down our starboard side, firing and killing men as she went. We opened up with our six-inch gun, but things were happening so quickly by that time that our men couldn't seem to hit the attacking boat but managed to make it submerge only to come up again about two miles away.

"As our steering gear and wireless were useless, we were at the mercy of the enemy, but kept firing at the submarine. Every shot the enemy fired hit. He tried to hit our after gun, which he finally did, killing four of the men and disabling the gun. We were then helpless, and he began shelling us with shrapnel, killing men right and left. How I escaped death I don't know. Men fell all around me and the deck was covered with blood and with dead and dying men. I know there were at least 150 men lying in pools of blood. All of our boats that had been lowered were swamped, and the men in them were drowned. There was only one boat left, and we lowered that and put in the Captain and two other badly wounded men and fourteen soldiers, and lowered it into the water, and that was the only boat I know of which got away safely.

"There were then about twenty-five men left on the then sinking ship. I did not know but that I would be hit by a shell any minute, as the ship was being punctured with holes from bow to stern. The ship was full of holes. I did not fear death, and I knew it was only a matter of a few minutes and I would be in the water.

"About that time two fellows beside me were killed. I got hit in the leg but as I could stand up I didn't wait to see how badly. About that time, perhaps at 7:30, the sub sent a torpedo into us. We were sinking, but I guess he didn't think he was killing us off fast enough, so he was hurrying it up. The torpedo hit us amid-

ships and broke the steam pipes and the steam was going everywhere.

"I knew I must get ready to jump overboard with just a life
preserver on. I went aft and picked up a piece of wood and as
water was only a few feet from the after deck I was just going to
step off. I knew it would only be a matter of a few hours and I
would die of exposure. I looked around and saw a raft, which had
not been pushed off, and went up forward and climbed up to it.
There were some ten fellows all lying down beside it, and I asked
them why they were lying there and as I spoke I found out the
reason. The sub was trying to shoot us off. It was just cold-
blooded murder, that's all.

"Well, I got the fellows up, as we were sinking pretty fast,
and after we had put three wounded men on top of the raft we
pushed it off the top some twenty feet from the water and
jumped over after it and climbed on and pulled the three
wounded men up from the water as the raft tipped over.

"We were none too soon, for we were only ten feet away
when the bow came straight up in the air and the *Ticonderoga*
shot to the depths. There we were on an open raft 1,600 miles
from any land and the wind blowing hard and a rough sea running which washed over us and made it difficult even to hold on.

"Now I can tell you, Mother, that things looked pretty bad; it
seemed to us to be simply a case of waiting until overtaken by
death. We got no wireless out, the convoy was miles ahead, and
the sub lying around. The lifeboat was about a mile to the wind-
ward of us. I saw the sub go up to her and found out afterward
that they wanted the Captain, the Chief Engineer, and the gunner.
The fellows lied and said the Captain was dead. The Huns then

tied the boat to the stern of the sub and started ahead, intending to drown them all, but by a chance of luck the line carried away and although the Germans called them back they didn't go.

"The sub then fired three shots at the boat but did not hit it. She then came on to us on the raft and tied us alongside, covering us with their revolvers. I expected by be shot any minute. They took a moving picture of us and took our officer prisoner. When they asked me who I was I thought sure I was a goner.

"They finally eased us off and we drifted away, and even though I knew I would die before long I was mighty glad to get away from them.

"The lifeboat kept drifting nearer and about four o'clock that afternoon came alongside and five of us got in the boat. We tried to get a line to the raft, but couldn't. I was then wet through and very cold, but was some better off than on the raft. There were three very badly wounded men, and one died a little while after I got in the boat and we had to throw the poor fellow overboard. Mr. Ringelman, an ensign, and I were the only two in the boat who knew how to handle it, and you can believe me we had a hard job to keep it from swamping.

"I took account of our supplies and found we only had eight gallons of water, some canned apricots and pineapples, and a case of hardtack. We decided that all we could give a day was one apricot and two spoonfuls of juice twice a day. I will not go into details of the next four days, but will tell you of our sufferings when I get home. . . .

"Your ship wrecked boy, George."

They drifted in that lifeboat for five days before the British ship the *Moorish Prince* picked them up. Three days later, the survivors were transferred to the *Grampian*, a faster ship bound for New York, since neither of the British vessels had medical facilities.

Of the twenty-two men who floated in that lifeboat, fourteen died.

Of the approximatly 240 men aboard the *Ticonderoga*, my grandfather was one of eight survivors. Other newspaper accounts support George Tapply's report, although theirs are less understated than his in suggesting that the chief quartermaster's courage and heroism and commitment to duty were extraordinary.

When he arrived at the Army hospital in Brooklyn, George Tapply learned that his "dear little wife" had died of influenza.

After he recovered from his wounds (which he'd downplayed in his letter to his mother), George returned to his hometown of Waltham. Since a single man could not, in those days, be expected to raise a boy by himself, he found families in Waltham for his young son to board with until he could find him a proper mother.

When George remarried, he brought his son home. But the marriage was a disaster. It ended quickly in divorce and again the boy was boarded out.

The families who took Horace in treated him well, he recalls, and his father did his best to raise his son, albeit from a distance. Ray Morse, one of those who boarded Dad, introduced him to fox hunting and trout fishing.

Nevertheless, Horace (he got the nickname "Tap" in college, for which he has been forever grateful), knew no secure and stable home in his childhood. Life, Dad learned at an early age, was stern and earnest indeed.

CHAPTER THREE

PARTNERS

I became Dad's hunting and fishing partner as soon as I proved I could keep up with him in the woods, take my fair turn at the oars, and keep my mouth shut from the back seat. He didn't abandon his adult companions. But somehow he must have made it clear to them that Tap's boy went with Tap whether they liked it or not.

My excellence at being seen and not heard, I'm sure, helped make it work, but I still find it admirable that Dad's long-time partners — Put Putnam, Gorham Cross, Harold Blaisdell, and all the others — accepted me with good grace. I spoke to them, as Dad so often reminded me, only when spoken to, but they generally spoke to me enough to make me feel comfortable in their company. I can't imagine that Dad's old companions wouldn't have preferred to have Tap to themselves. But they never made me feel like an intruder.

Dad did not believe a kid should call adults by their first names, even when they fished and hunted together. So I called them "uncle" — "Uncle Put" and "Uncle Harold" — a habit I continued well into my own adulthood, even when their kids were calling my father "Tap." Those men I didn't know very well I called "Mister," although I found it easier not to call them any-thing at all—which I generally managed, since I had perfected the art of not being heard.

Uncle Put took to calling me "Harm"—something about keeping fragile pieces of fishing equipment out of harm's way in a canoe.

Dad and Uncle Harold carried on long and sometimes acri-monious debates during the long drives over Vermont backroads to places like Otter Creek, the White River, the Battenkill, and Lake Champlain. Times like these, I knew, were important tests for my skill at being not heard, and I absorbed a great deal from the back seat. I clearly heard how intelligent grownups talked—and listened—to each other, for one thing.

Mostly, though, Dad and I made a twosome. We spent virtually every weekend from April through November on the road. There were few corners in the northern half of New England that we didn't explore in search of trout or bass or ruffed grouse. Once my legs had grown long enough to reach the pedals, I did the driving. I would estimate that I logged 20,000 road miles be-fore I reached the legal age of sixteen to go for my license. Dad liked to say, "Experience is the best teacher," and he believed it was his parental obligation to provide me with experience in all important matters—fly casting, shotgun handling, and auto-mobile driving.

So we were partners. But neither of us ever forgot who was the kid and who the parent. Although terms such as "friend" and "pal" come to my mind now, when I was growing up, Dad was my father, my elder, who by simple virtue of his adulthood com-manded my respect. The line never became fuzzy for either of us.

I was always acutely aware of the fact that he did not curse in front of me (he didn't curse much anyway, I quickly learned), nor would I dare utter a "damn" within his hearing, although that word (and several other even more useful ones) rolled easily off my tongue in the company of my peers. Fathers and sons did not talk to each other that way, even if fishing and hunting partners sometimes did.

I don't recall his ever expressing anger toward me, or criticizing me, although I gave him ample opportunity for both. Uncle Put didn't call me "Harm" idly. I was eager, impetuous, and — Dad's word — "heedless," which often enough translated into careless treatment of fragile equipment. Since we fished almost exclusively with split-bamboo fly rods when I was growing up, the results were predictable. Dad had an enormous collection of bamboo rods, many of which would be prized by today's collectors. I've recently looked over what's left of them (he's given away dozens over the years). Virtually all of them have shortened and repaired tip sections — evidence that at one time or another they got in Harm's way.

Once I heedlessly slammed the car door while Dad was still backing out his strung-up fly rod. It shattered in mid-section. Dad gazed down at the totaled rod for a moment, then smiled at me and said, "I'd hate to tell you how many rods I've broken in my life."

"Errors are part of the game," he liked to say, a philosophy consistent with his belief that the best learning takes place through experience. Dad generally refrained from telling me how to do things. Partners did not instruct each other. He believed in experience, trial and error, figuring things out for one's self.

Occasionally he might say, "I do it this way," and if I directly asked his advice or instruction, he gave it fully and freely. But his primary teaching method was to allow me plenty of opportunities to try and to err. I had a vast appetite for trying and an absolute genius for erring. Perhaps there are more efficient ways to learn. But I did learn. And Dad was philosophical about the inevitable errors his educational theory produced.

I once rear-ended another car while driving the two of us home from an afternoon of trout fishing on the Squannicook. It was a clear case of heedlessness — I was driving too fast, too close to the vehicle in front of me, and had failed to react to the flash of brake lights. I was fourteen, an outlaw driver two years shy of my license. Dad knew the experience would serve as a powerful teacher, and that he didn't need to criticize me or tell me what I'd done wrong. His only comment was: "Accidents happen."

The next weekend when we went fishing I refused to drive. "I don't feel like it," was all I said, but in fact I had lost my confidence.

Dad shrugged and took the wheel. But when we had unstrung our rods and loaded our gear into the car at the end of the day, he said, "Want to drive?"

"No," I said, "that's all right."

He smiled at me and said, "I think you should drive."

I drove home — very heedfully — and made it without mishap.

After a particularly egregious act of destructive heedlessness, Dad would roll his eyes and call me "a Bill in a China shop." This was as close to anger or criticism as he ever came.

Dad encouraged me to speak candidly with him by taking

my thoughts seriously and refraining from judging me. For the most part I felt comfortable doing so, although I avoided those particularly embarrassing issues that whirled in my pubescent brain like swarms of caddisflies. My mother the nurse was my source of practical information on hormonal questions.

I suspect that Dad sensed my reticence on these matters and took his paternal obligations seriously (although I can imagine Mum telling him, "You really *should* talk to Bill, you know"), because on one long road trip to some distant New England trout river he segued cleverly from an account of a Newfoundland fishing excursion into a long and detailed narrative of the life history of the Atlantic salmon. He admired this fish above all others, it was clear. It leaves its familiar home river at a young age, confronts the perils of the sea for three or four years, grows large, then returns as a mature adult to its natal place.

It's a journey of thousands of miles through treacherous seas and over great waterfalls. Salmon are guided by a mysterious navigational instinct and fueled by the overwhelming, single-minded urge to reproduce. Nothing can stop hen and buck salmon from their rendezvous back home. The female builds her redd and lays her eggs. The male lies by her side and fertilizes them in a cloud of milt. Soon little parr are born, grow into smolts, and after a year or two they head to sea to recapitulate the cycle.

"You know what milt is," Dad said, not quite a question.

"Sure."

"Oh. Okay. Good."

Of course, I thought he was talking about fish. Unlike Mum, Dad had always seemed bashful when it came to matters of the flesh. He had explained to me the significance of a mayfly spinner fall—strictly in the context of selecting the right fly to match what the trout were eating. He had led me to field edges in March to witness the elaborate courtship rituals of the woodcock. But it didn't occur to me until sometime later that his version of the requisite paternal "birds and bees" sermon would naturally use a fish for its dominant metaphor.

Usually, though, it was democratic give and take. I cannot imagine another father and son spending more time together—in the car, in a canoe, around campfires, in restaurants and motel rooms. Virtually every weekend from April through November throughout my childhood, Dad and I hunted birds and fish in New England—sometimes with his adult companions, but mostly just the two of us. We talked constantly. We debated Red Sox prospects (always bleak in those days, though Dad was more of a realist than I). I pumped him for fishing and hunting lore. I loved to get him talking about places he had been, fish he had caught, people he had known.

His own childhood was a subject that remained ancient and mysterious to me. He referred to it rarely, and then only in a cursory way. I never asked him about it. I suppose I sensed that if he wanted to, or if he thought it would interest me, he'd talk about it. Besides, he had plenty of other fascinating tales to tell.

As much from his example as from his words, I absorbed a value system and philosophy that remain operative for me still—the poetry of fly fishing, love of nature's mysteries, respect for all wild creatures—along with more fundamental and important values such as honesty, self-respect, humility, cooperation, and family.

I sensed that he respected my opinion and was genuinely interested in hearing it. We learned to disagree amiably. I'm a middle-aged man now (though still occasionally heedless, I admit), and Dad's into his ninth decade. We continue to enjoy our philosophical discussions. Now we debate politics and economics and religion the way he and Uncle Harold used to up in the front seat. Our conversations often become heated, but never personal, although they sometimes upset my mother, who insists on calling them "arguments."

Dad is thirty years my elder. In a lifetime, I haven't closed the gap by a day, and both of us still know which is the kid and which the father.

In a trout stream or a grouse cover or a canoe, though, we functioned as cooperative equals from the beginning. We took turns, we divided the labor, and we shared credit for whatever fish we caught or birds we shot, because that's how partnerships worked.

You couldn't predict a grouse's escape route, but if two men plotted and executed a proper strategy, one of them would get a shot. It didn't matter which one. I learned to enjoy the success that our teamwork produced, regardless of who got the shooting, and I soon understood that it was proper for either of us, when reporting to other hunters, to say "*We* got three woodcock and two grouse today."

At first I suspected that this was Dad's way of sheltering a pitifully inept wingshot (me) from the obvious comparison, for in his day Dad was a deadly grouse and woodcock marksman. On a good day I might have scratched down one of those three woodcock and none of the grouse. But the law of averages legislates that the day would eventually come when my game bag was heavier than Dad's. When it finally happened, I listened carefully to his account of that day's hunt. "We had a good day," he told the gathering at the Valley Hotel that night. "Five woodcock and three grouse."

I learned, too, that when the man in the bow landed a trout, he ought to know enough to glance over his shoulder and say to the man with the paddle, "Good guiding, partner." We caught fish in the first-person plural, as well.

We still do it that way.

CHAPTER FOUR

INVISIBLE WRITING

*A*nother of Dad's aphorisms: "Any job worth doing is worth doing well."

The operative word here was "job," a synonym, more or less, for "chore" or "unpleasant task." Fly casting and wing shooting were not jobs. These activities could be done well or poorly and it didn't matter very much. Besides, you didn't need an aphorism to inspire you to try to do them well. Accurate casting and shooting produced their own rewards.

Heedless boys — especially those who had earned the nickname "Harm" — needed to be reminded that it took very little extra effort to mow a lawn neatly or to wash all the dirt off the family car. Even if nobody else noticed — and the significant thing about "jobs" was that people tended to notice them only when they were poorly done — a person should take pride in everything he did.

Dad's jobs in one way or the other always involved writing which, he persistently maintained, was about the hardest work known to man. I didn't buy it, any more than I deep-down agreed that life was "stern and earnest."

Weeding the gardens and shoveling snow were hard.

Writing was like fly casting — natural and fun.

In the beginning, writing came easy to me. My teachers always loved my stories. They came back to me with comments such as, "Wonderful descriptions," or, "Excellent use of vocabulary words."

When I showed them to Dad, he just smiled and said, "Another 'A'. Congratulations."

I noticed that he never had much to say about the stories themselves. But what could be said about an "A" paper? Dad was a writer. He knew talent when he saw it. I figured he was proud of me, glad I had inherited his good writing genes. I was a natural.

In my junior year I was assigned to Mr. Cheever's English class. The older kids warned me: Mr. Cheever was tough and mean. "Miniver," they called him behind his back, after the Edward Arlington Robinson poem he always made them read. "Miniver Cheevy, child of scorn." Old Miniver did not give "A"s.

Of course, he hadn't seen my stuff yet.

First impressions, I knew, were important. So I worked especially hard on my first assignment for Mr. Cheever. I took extra pains to create elaborate descriptions and sprinkle in lots of good vocabulary words. It was the best thing I'd ever done, I knew, but just to be sure I showed it to Dad.

"You haven't handed it in yet?" he said.

I shook my head. "Mr. Cheever's a hard marker," I said. "I just want to be sure it's perfect."

"So you want my opinion?"

"Sure."

He arched his eyebrows. "Or do you want me to tell you it's fine?"

"Your opinion," I said, which I felt confident amounted to the same thing.

He read it with a red pen in his hand. Fifteen minutes later he handed it back to me. Every page had eight or ten words circled in red.

"Verbs," said Dad.

"Huh?"

"You depend too much on the verb 'to be.' Use active verbs. Put them to work. Find the right verb and you can eliminate all these flabby adverbs and fancy adjectives." He pointed with the tip of his pen at those excellent vocabulary words I had strung together to make my wonderfully descriptive passages.

I nodded. "Okay," I said. "Verbs. Otherwise, how is it?"

"There are some other things," he said. "But first, the verbs."

I took the paper back and found some good verbs in my *Thesaurus*. Mr. Cheever gave my story a "C+". "Don't try to impress me," was his only comment.

I showed Dad the draft of my next story. "Help, please," I said.

"You're sure?"

"I'm desperate," I said. "Miniver's tough."

He smiled. "That's progress."

I watched his face while he read my story. He gave nothing away. When he finished, he looked up at me. "You've certainly attended to your verbs," he said. He jabbed at the paper. "Where'd you get this one?"

"*Nictitate*? I learned it last year."

"Good word," said Dad. "What's it mean?"

"Wink."

"That's a better word," he said. "Who're you trying to impress?"

I smiled. "Old Miniver.'

"And?"

"He mentioned the same thing."

Dad handed my paper to me. "Invisible writing," he said. "Understand?"

"No."

"Don't try to impress your reader with how cleverly you write. These fancy words, all these adjectives and adverbs and *vocabulary* words" — he pronounced the word "vocabulary" as if it meant "disgusting human waste product" — "all they do is call attention to you. You don't want your reader aware of your writing at all. If you do your job, you'll have them thinking about your ideas, your arguments, your characters, or whatever it is you're trying to communicate. If someone tells you, 'Wow, that's great writing,' you know you've failed."

"You mean all my other teachers . . . ?"

He shrugged. "You've been getting bad advice."

"Well," I said, "I appreciate yours."

"You do?"

"Yes, sir."

"That's a good start," he said.

Another time he said, "Tighten it up. Find the one right word and you can get rid of a dozen wrong ones."

"Yeah," I said, "but then my stories'll be too short."

"Short," said Dad, "is good."

For the rest of my high school career — I got Mr. Cheever the next year, too — I shared the drafts of my papers with Dad. He always found something new to criticize. Invisible writing, I learned, demanded conciseness and clarity, along with precise, unpretentious, and hard-working verbs. It didn't come easily to me. I labored over my stories. I tried to anticipate Dad's criticisms.

"Writing isn't that much fun anymore," I said to him after one of our sessions.

"Fun?" He rolled his eyes. "Writing is hard work, if you intend to take it seriously. But a job worth doing — "

"Right," I said.

He smiled. "It's ironic. But with writing, the more you learn about it, the harder it gets."

"I guess I'm beginning to see that."

"But you're taking it seriously, huh?"

"I want to get it right."

"Maybe we'll make a writer of you yet, then."

For years I had watched Dad at his typewriter without really understanding what I was seeing. Every night after dinner he trudged down to his basement office to work ("work" was a synonym for "write" in my home). He hunched over his ancient Underwood in a gray haze of pipesmoke, his fingers poised, staring at the yellow paper he used for rough drafts. At unpredictable times his fingers — two on each hand plus his right thumb for the space bar — would suddenly begin to hammer the keys. Then, just as abruptly, he'd stop and stare at the yellow paper. His shoulders would slump for a moment before he'd rip the paper from his machine, ball it up, and toss it over his shoulder onto the floor behind him.

Then he'd roll in a clean sheet of paper and stare at it. And at the end of an evening of work, his office floor would lie buried under an ankle-deep layer of balled-up yellow paper.

Now it was beginning to make sense. Writing involved more than stringing together good vocabulary words. Writing was a job. Doing it well — making it invisible — had to be the most painfully difficult occupation known to man.

———

As a schoolboy I won dimes from my friends by betting them that I was in *Who's Who*. Of course, my name appeared under Dad's listing. When I was growing up, H.G. Tapply was one of the big names in outdoor writing and publishing.

Dad put himself through Northeastern University during the Depression years by working in a mince-meat factory, writing sports for the college newspaper, stringing local college sports for the *Globe*, and a number of other jobs. After graduating with a business degree in 1932, he and a buddy drove cross-country ("We kept the needle on thirty-five," he remembers, "because we believed that was the most efficient gas-mileage speed and we were both virtually broke") to visit with Dad's cousins in Coronado, California. There he quickly picked up a job with the *Coronado Journal*, a semi-weekly paper. "I did whatever I was asked to do," he recalls, "and even what I wasn't asked to do, which latter included a silly column titled 'And So to Press,' mainly about unimportant doings around town." He still maintains that small-town newspaper work offers the best possible experience for the aspiring writer.

While in California, he came across a copy of *National Sportsman* magazine, which was published in Boston. He wrote a letter to its editor-in-chief (and also editor of the companion magazine, *Hunting & Fishing*,) William Harnden Foster. "I'll be returning to Boston soon," wrote young Tap, "and when I do I'm going to come in and ask you for a job."

He wrote two or three more letters to Foster. "Just to remind you that when I get home I'll be asking you for a job."

And when he did return East, he presented himself to Bill Foster at 108 Massachusetts Avenue. He was not hired.

A few weeks later Dad showed up at the office again. Sorry.

But his third or fourth visit coincided with Edmund Ware Smith's retirement as managing editor, so Foster hired the eager young man as an "editorial assistant." His starting salary was $18 per week. He began doing what he calls "scut work," uninspiring jobs that he undoubtedly believed were worth doing well, and soon he found himself reviewing manuscripts, reading proof, editing copy, re-titling stories, and writing photo captions. "Anything Bill asked me to do," he recalls.

During that time the young editorial assistant published his first story, a fox-hunting piece called "Rabbits Seem Kinda Small" —an embarrassingly bad title, he agrees. Foster made him rewrite it thirteen times, Dad remembers, "and it was still a terrible story, more like a high-school composition. He published it, I'm sure, just to encourage me."

Sometime in 1936 while visiting a friend in the hospital he met a pretty young nurse-in-training. "Actually, he wasn't that close a friend," Dad recalls, "but I visited him every chance I could until I got up the nerve to ask his nurse if she'd like to go fishing with me." She proved to be a terrific sport, and in 1938 Tap married Muriel Morgridge.

They honeymooned in the wilds of Maine with Dad's friends George and Marian Smith, who ran a sporting camp on Sysladobsis Lake. After closing the landlocked salmon season on Dobsis, the two couples motored twelve miles up the lake and portaged three miles into Fourth Lake Machias. There they lived for a week in George's one-room cabin and caught arm-long pickerel on Dardevle spoons.

"It was a small cabin," Dad told me. "One-holer out back, kerosene lamps, wood stove, water from the lake. The four of us slept in bunk beds. I recall one night your mother whispered 'I love you' to me, and from the darkness I heard Marian say to George, 'Now what do you suppose she sees in him?' "

"Oh, Tap," says Mum. "She did not."

Dad shrugs, conceding that his story is apocryphal. "We ate illegal moose that George had shot, I remember that. He kept it cool in the lake."

"It was venison," says Mum.

They finished up their Maine honeymoon woodcock hunting in the rain. They had no dogs, so Mum and Marian were recruited to thrash through the soaking alder runs to drive out the birds to the men.

Both of my parents remember their honeymoon fondly.

H. G. Tapply was appointed managing editor of *National Sports-man/Hunting & Fishing* in 1935 (at the age of twenty-five), editor in 1936, and in 1940 he became editor of *Outdoors* magazine, which job he held until the magazine was purchased by a Chicago group in 1950. During those fifteen years he bought stories from just about every prominent outdoor writer of that generation. Many of them became his lifelong friends and sporting companions. When I was growing up, I often had to turn over my bedroom to house guests such as Lee Wulff, Ed Zern, Harold Blaisdell, Joe Bates, and Henry Davis. Dad fished with Ted Williams and Curt Gowdy. Talk around our dining room table was heady for a fanatical young hunter and fisherman. Sometimes I even got to tag along on their hunting and fishing excursions.

Dad wrote dozens of stories during these years, mostly under pseudonyms such as H.T. Gardner, H.G. Traill, and Gardner Grant. Hy Gunn was the name he used for the "scores and scores" of articles he wrote about skeet, the new sport that Bill Foster, his first boss, co-invented.

In 1939 Dad, Ollie Rodman, and Hugh Grey (then Dad's assistant editor) put together an eight-page newsletter they called *Salt Water Sportsman*. It was printed by Banker & Tradesman Press, whose owner, Gorham Cross ("Grampa Grouse," he called himself) became Dad's grouse-shooting partner until Cross's death in 1955. *SWS* was eventually purchased by Henry Lyman, who remains its Publisher Emeritus to this day.

In 1946 Dad published his first book, *Tackle Tinkering*. *The Fly Tyer's Handbook* appeared in 1949. Both are now collectors' items, of course, and nearly fifty years of technology have rendered much of their wisdom obsolete. The section on rod repair deals only with split bamboo, and considerable attention is given to the problem of handling and caring for gut leaders. An entire page of text is devoted to shopping for and selecting junglecock necks.

But the prose is sharp and precise — I challenge anyone to write clearer directions for tying a whip finish or spinning deerhair than those found in the *Handbook*.

These books are full of the kinds of tips, informational nuggets, and home-made gadgets that later became synonymous with "Tap." Both volumes are still models of "invisible writing."

When he left *Outdoors*, (declining to move his family to Chicago to continue as its editor), Dad became a freelancer. During this period Hugh Grey, who by then had become editor-in-chief of *Field & Stream*, suggested he start a column called, naturally, "Tap's Tips," which, along with his "The Sportsman's Notebook" (a 500-word column), would be monthly features in the magazine for the next thirty-five years. The Tips are still being reprinted in *Field & Stream* today.

In spite of the millions of words he wrote and edited in his career, in hunting and fishing circles Dad was — and remains — reknowned and revered primarily as the Tap of "Tap's Tips."

Dad did not believe freelance writing provided enough income security to raise a young family, so after a year of it ("during which time I did an awful lot of hunting and fishing"), he joined a Boston advertising firm. But he continued to write his column for *Field & Stream* in the evenings. Every month for thirty-five years he composed six miniature articles, each a complete essay containing useful, original, and timely advice or information for the outdoorsman — how to select the best snowshoe design, how to prevent campfire soot from blackening cooking utensils, how to pluck porcupine quills from a bird dog's nose, how to revive matted dry flies.

He published twenty-five hundred tips altogether, I calculate. Every one of them contained between forty and fifty words — five typed lines. No more, no less.

Writing a fifty-word tip, he maintained, was harder than writing a 500-word Notebook article. Every tip had to be a masterpiece of conciseness and clarity — a complete tale, with a beginning, a middle, and an end, in fifty words or less. He enjoyed no margin for error. Every word, literally, counted. He could afford to squander none of them. One of "Tap's Tips" simply and efficiently did its job: It conveyed information.

People thought of Tap as an expert outdoorsman. True to his nature, Dad rejected the label "expert" out of hand. But when I learned to appreciate what he did, I found it ironic that nobody seemed to consider him an expert writer.

But it gratified him. It meant, he said, that he'd done his job well: He'd succeeded in making his writing invisible.

———

Dad's advice got me a few grudging "A"s from Mr. Cheever and sustained me through college term papers. His example steered me into a career that didn't require me to write.

I resisted the writing impulse for a long time, and when I finally gave in to it, I found myself fully prepared for those long paralyzed moments of staring at my typewriter, trying to make my writing disappear. I could rip out a sheet of paper, ball it up, and toss it over my shoulder without flinching.

I wrote to please the critic in my head, whose persistent voice kept repeating things like, "Short is good," and, "Who're you trying to impress?"

I believed that writing was a job worth doing well.

———

To this day I often ask Dad to take his red pen to my work. "You really want my opinion?" he asks.

"Sure."

Fifteen minutes later he looks up at me, smiles, and says, "Verbs."

CHAPTER FIVE

WILD TROUT

*T*he first fishing memory I can coax out of Dad is of a native brook trout he caught in Wells, Maine. "I ran all the way back to Gram's with it so she could cook it for me," he remembers. The year of Dad's sojourn in Wells was 1918, when his father was criss-crossing the North Atlantic and his mother was nursing influenza victims in Massachusetts.

That trout, he admits, was probably not the first fish he ever caught. But it was the first memorable one.

I derricked a sunfish out of the Charles River when I was three or four. Dad verifies this as my first official fish and has a black-and-white photograph to immortalize the momentous occasion. I'm wearing what he calls "rompers." He once embarrassed me unforgivably by showing this photo to one of my high-school girl friends, though he did have the good judgment not to open the album to the page with the pictures of baby Bill lying bareass on the bearskin rug.

I went on to catch thousands of sunfish (we kids called them "kivvers" or "kibbies") — and horned pout and yellow perch, and lesser numbers of crappies (which we called "calico bass") and pond shiners and bluegills and even a few stunted largemouth bass, skinny pickerel, and twisting eels—from the tepid little ponds within bicycle range of my neighborhood. I fished exclusively with worms and fly rod. I became adept at roll-casting firmly enough to lob my worm out to the mysterious depths where I could not see the bottom, and yet gently enough to prevent the worm from flying off my hook. I never tired of waiting for that delicious moment when the leader began to vibrate and twitch and then the line jerked and slithered through the guides. Even a sunfish the size of a Ritz cracker had enough strength to tug out line, so until I tightened and reared back on the rod, I could—and always did—hope that some kind of monster had taken my worm. It never was a monster, of course, but no sunfish, however stunted, disappointed me. It could have been a monster, and the next one might be, and that was enough.

Time, back then, was an infinite commodity, and I spent most of mine fishing, or dreaming about fishing.

Actually, I still do, and I still love that moment when the leader begins to twitch, and I still can believe that this time a monster has bitten. If it's true that "Allah does not deduct from the allotted time of man those hours spent in fishing," then I am still a child.

But of all those countless thousands of local panfish I caught, not a single one was memorable, and were it not for a yellowed old photograph, not a single one would be remembered.

Trout were—and still are—memorable. I can remember my first trout, my first dry-fly trout, my first nymph-caught trout, my first big trout, my first western trout, and many particularly difficult trout. I have no such vivid recollections of other species.

Dad learned trout fishing from Ray Morse, with whom he

boarded after his mother's death. They prowled local waters such as Hobbs Brook and Stony Brook armed with fly rods and worms, and they caught little native brookies.

I started the same way, although by then the only brook we knew of in our part of eastern Massachusetts that still held natives was a little rill two towns away. It was too small and remote even to have a name. Its anonymity, of course, only heightened its appeal. If it had no name, I could believe that Dad, who could keep a secret, had discovered it.

I could walk or pedal my bike to a nearby panfish pond anytime. But trout fishing was an Occasion precisely because it was not local. Trout were special because I fished for them only with Dad, and because they were scarce and wild and hard to catch and beautiful.

We visited our secret little brook only two or three times a season, in April, before the larger rivers that Dad liked to fish cleared up and mayflies began to hatch. We dug worms in the morning—a ceremony of its own. Dad said we only needed a dozen or so. He was right, of course, because we only expected to get a few bites, but I insisted that we gather a hundred, on the theory that you never knew when you'd hit it just right, and you certainly didn't want to run out of bait.

Our brook meandered slow and inscrutable through a vast boggy meadow. Dad nosed the car into a barway and we had to walk through the pine woods for fifteen or twenty minutes to get to the brook. On those early days of spring we sometimes still found dirty patches of old snow in shadowy places under the evergreens. The swampy April breezes carried the faint mingled aromas of pine needles and thawing earth and rotting vegetation. The willows and alders and young hardwoods were just beginning to bud, but the trees showed no leaves, and it was a dark black-and-white place hidden from the sun by the hills and the pines. We usually heard a grouse drumming in the distance. It sounded like a balky old engine trying to get started. Sometimes we flushed a migrating woodcock. We studied the mud for tracks of raccoons, mink, muskrat, and deer.

I knew even back then that trout places could be as alluring as trout fishing.

A half-grown boy could jump across our brook in most places. Its currents were barely noticeable. For so narrow a little rill, it ran deep against undercut banks and under blowdown. Its stained tea-colored water obscured its mysteries. You had to intepret its surface to figure out what lay underneath. Trout, Dad said, lurked in deep protected places. They survived because predators such as mink and herons and kingfishers could not catch them.

Most trout, of course, did not survive. Those that managed it were the smartest and wariest and swiftest, and those were the ones that lived long enough to reproduce and pass along their smart and wary and swift genes. That's why trout were hard to catch.

We are trout predators, Dad said. We must be smarter and warier than the trout if we should hope to get one to bite.

I loved the idea of being a trout predator. It seemed to make the trout at least my equal. I liked knowing that I had to be as stealthy as a mink or a heron to catch one. You didn't just roll-cast a worm out into the water and wait for a trout to come along and twitch at your line. You had to figure out where a trout might be hiding, and you had to stalk him without his knowing it. You had to drift your worm to him in such a way that he would mistake it for a natural bait and decide, despite all of his survival-tuned instincts, to eat it.

This trout fishing did not involve sophisticated equipment or complex strategies or esoteric science. It was basic, but subtle, too. Fishing for native brook trout in this wild little brook, I understood, was a kind of hunting. It was, as worm-dunking for panfish was not, *real* fishing. Wild brook trout were *real* fish.

We hit the brook somewhere in the middle of the swamp and fished it back toward the car. I would start in and Dad would circle the alders and willows to a spot fifty feet or so downstream of me. He'd hang his handkerchief on a bush and begin there. When I fished my way down to the handkerchief, I'd take it, circle around Dad, and hang it where I resumed.

We fished as slowly and precisely and stealthily as herons. We crouched on the boggy banks and hunkered behind bushes, thrusting out our rods to drop our baits so that they would drift deep and tight to the undercuts, and it took a half hour or more to cover the distance down to the handkerchief.

Thus we leap-frogged each other, always within shouting distance, always fishing virgin water. It was at once solitary and companionable.

As near as we could tell, no one else had ever fished there. We never found footprints or cigarette butts on the boggy banks, and this, as much as the trout that lived in it, gave our brook its special romance.

We used small dry-fly hooks and light leaders. The currents moved slowly enough that we had no need to pinch on split shot. The worm, hooked just once behind its head, drifted free and wiggly when we swung it into the water. To catch a trout, the bait had to arrive precisely onto the trout's platter, for I learned that while they readily ate what came directly to them, these skittish little fish would not venture far from their protected hideouts to feed. Those heedless ones that did had already made dinner for a mink or kingfisher.

They took so delicately that you had to stare hard at the place where your leader entered the water to detect it. It was a hesitation, perhaps a tiny twitch, no more. These trout did not pick up a worm and flee with it the way panfish did.

Set the hook instantly, Dad said. Two reasons: first, trout had an uncanny instinct for detecting something unnatural and would drop it quickly; and, second, we wanted to hook them lightly in the lips in order to retain the option of returning them to the water.

In fact, we imposed a kind of slot-limit on ourselves and hardly ever kept a trout from our brook. They ran so small that a six-incher earned our admiration and comment. The rare seven- or eight-incher was a meal and worth bringing home. Anything bigger was a trophy too rare and precious to kill.

They were stained dark and coppery like the water where they lived. Their spots glittered like drops of fresh blood inside sky-blue haloes, and their fins were edged with ivory. A six-incher in my hand felt cold and muscular and wild. I believed then — and I still do — that a small native brook trout is nature's most beautiful and elusive creation. Catching one initiates the lucky boy into exalted company. It makes him a mink or a heron — a hunter, a creature of Nature himself. No experience in my life, with the exception of watching the birth of my children, has been as transcendent for me as catching wild little trout from that wild little brook.

Usually the lift of the rod brought them flipping and wiggling out of the water. But once I hooked one that bowed my fly rod, and when we were linked I felt his powerful panicky surge and saw the underwater flash of his broad golden side. Then he snapped my leader.

To this day I don't know if Dad believed me when I reported having hooked such a large trout. For days I mourned its loss. Landing that trout would have made me a hero. Instead, I believed I was a boy whose father suspected him of tall tales.

Had I landed him, I would have been tempted to kill that trout and bring it home and show it off to my mother and my friends and prove to Dad what a gifted predator I had become. But I gradually came to realize that I preferred knowing that monster trout (it was probably a twelve-incher) continued to live in our brook. And Dad always claimed he believed me.

I've caught a lot of wild trout since those April days with Dad — Snake River cutthroats, Montana rainbows, Labrador brookies — fish whose ancestry extends back before recorded history, whose progenitors inhabited those same waters long before a man with a spear hunted them. Many of them were not mere twelve-inchers but certifiable trophies. They came hard, and at great expense. Catching them demanded refined skills, specialized equipment, expertise, patience, and luck.

They were trout, and therefore memorable.

But no trout are more memorable for me than those first wild little brookies, and no single trout lives more clearly in my memory than that one monster twelve-incher that got away.

———

Even after I became addicted to fly casting and we had widened our fishing circle to encompass all of New England, Dad and I continued to visit our little brook every April. We did it ceremonially, just once a year, on the afternoon of Patriot's Day after the morning parade. We dug a can of worms (I continued to insist that we bring many more than we needed) and carried our fly rods through the woods to the place in the swamp that hid our private wild trout brook.

The day we found the surveyor's markers scattered through the swamp and along the margins of our brook was the last day we went there. I tore those orange stakes from the ground and heaved them into the woods, and Dad, uncharacteristically, did not chide me for my vandalism.

He didn't help me rip up the stakes, either, although I believe he would have if he thought it would help. He knew instantly what I had instinctively realized: Progress had found our brook, and Nature, even with our help, was no match for its implacable force.

We fished the brook that April day, and the trout were as abundant as ever, although the monster did not bite. We caught no eight-inchers, but the little ones were coppery and wiggly and wild. We returned them all, even though we knew it was an act of quixotic futility. Our wild trout, we understood, were doomed.

Today I live less than a mile from that brook. The forest has been cut down, the hills leveled, the swamp drained. Suburban roads meander where our brook once flowed, and houses and garages and backyard swingsets sit where ruffed grouse once drummed in April.

Our brook flows straight and shallow through a concrete culvert. Its muddy banks bear the prints of children and dogs. Its water is dirt-stained and carries a faint septic odor, and the only thing that glitters in it is broken glass. Kids catch frogs and turtles from it, and wild mosquitoes reproduce themselves there as they have for eons.

It holds no wild brook trout.

CHAPTER SIX

THE SURE THING

*W*hen Dad retired from the advertising ratrace in 1967, he and Mum moved to the house on the hill in central New Hampshire where they still live. Lake Winnipesaukee nestles among the foothills half a mile away. From the sun porch, summer sailboats are visible and the afternoon sun glitters on the lake's surface, and on a clear day Mount Washington's white peak looms above the other Presidentials to the north.

Nearby Wolfeboro, the old resort town that the railroad built on the lake, is a popular retirement community. Mum has found plenty of bridge competition, and Dad's met some fishermen. Grandchildren descend on the house on Pond Road for Grandma's good cooking and a canoe ride on the lake with Grampa.

An excellent little sidehill partridge cover, a mix of poplar and alder, juniper and field edge, lies just over the stone wall behind Dad's vegetable garden. We hunted it the first year he lived there, but after that Dad decided he preferred to provide a sanctuary for the birds. Now we tromp through it unarmed, and although the poplars have grown taller, we still sometimes bump a grouse from the thick edges. We sneak out to the fields toward dusk in March to spy on woodcock courtship dances and to hear them peent.

Beaver Brook meanders through the alders and poplars at the foot of the hill on its way down to the lake. It's stocked with brook trout, and carryovers live — and perhaps reproduce — in the swampy upstream reaches. We've caught fingerling landlocked salmon from Beaver Brook.

Deer browse in Dad's backyard. Woodchucks browse in his garden. Foxes slink through the yard. We've found coyote tracks in the snow and moose prints in the mud up the street.

The house on Pond Road sits amidst our old grouse covers — the Owl Cover, the A-Frame, the Gun-on-the-Roof, and all the others that stretch southward until they merge with Burt Spiller's string of covers around Rochester. Knight's and Gilman's ponds hold largemouths and pickerel. The Pine River is stocked with trout.

Cardinals and grosbeaks, finches and titmice, and dozens of other species flock to Dad's homemade birdfeeders which, after years of Dad's tinkering and refining, are now almost squirrel-proof. The chickadees eat directly from his hand.

In the summer the hummingbirds buzz in the lilacs outside the kitchen window. A tame chipmunk named Charlie lives under the deck. He creeps up into Dad's lap to nibble donut crumbs.

Dad figures he's retired to heaven.

—————

Toward the end of May my phone rings. "They're on the beds," Dad announces.

"How's Thursday?"

He checks with Mum to be sure they don't have a bridge tournament or house gues scheduled (most of the house guests seem to come in May, when the Winnipesaukee small-mouths are on their spawning beds), then says, "Come early. Stay late."

For the first decade or so after Mum and Dad moved to Pond Road, Lake Winnipesaukee gave us what might have been the best smallmouth bass fishing in New England. It's a big, deep, cold-water lake, better known for its salmon and lake trout, and in those years few people fished it for bass.

The best time came toward the end of May, when the water had warmed enough to bring the spawn-minded smallmouths into the shallows, and before the hordes of summer vacationers arrived with their speedboats and water skis. We paddled the boulder-strewn shorelines in Dad's seventeen-foot Grumman. The fly caster in the bow probed the docks and dropoffs and points and coves with debarbed streamers or deerhair bugs. We looked for the sandy platters that marked the spawning beds guarded by the aggressive males. The paddler in the stern trolled a streamer and caught fewer fish. But he was more likely to hook one of the larger females.

On a good afternoon we caught bass until our arms ached. We kept count, because Mum demanded specific reports. On a typical three-hour outing we'd boat and release around fifty smallmouths. In those first several years, they averaged a couple of pounds, and we could generally count on nailing a four-pound female or two every time out.

———◦◦◦———

I loved baseball, but my favorite sport as a kid, "three-strikes-

and-out," was a fishing game. Dad and I played it on the Charles River on summer evenings after he came home from work.

The historic old Charles, where we fished it upriver from the dam by the Waltham Watch Factory, sprawled like a lake, with no discernable current or channel. The thickly wooded banks dropped steeply into the water, providing largemouths with shade, cover, depth, and all the frogs and baitfish and dragonflies and terrestrial insects they could eat. Lily pads clogged the coves, brush and tree limbs overhung the shorelines, and here and there big uprooted oaks lay in the water.

Bass-bug targets were everywhere.

The "three strikes" game assured equal fishing for the two of us and provided a powerful incentive for the paddler to position the canoe to the best advantage of the fisherman. The man with the fly rod cast to shoreline targets until he either landed a bass or missed three recognizable bass strikes. The occasional big bluegill or crappie that managed to get the bug into its mouth was a bonus fish that didn't count against us.

It was a team game, not a competitive one, although Dad and I took every opportunity to accuse each other of botching casts and missing strikes intentionally in order to keep the rod. Good guiding, I understood, earned me a quicker turn in the bow, and it didn't take me long to learn the satisfaction that comes from teamwork.

We found late-afternoon shade along a southern shoreline directly across from where we launched the canoe. We knew all the hotspots. A willow tree drooped its branches over the water, and a hard sidearm cast could bounce a deer-hair bug behind them into the shadows. A big bass always lived there. A little farther along lay a half-submerged fallen tree where on some days we might swap rods two or three times without moving.

For several years we clipped a pectoral fin on each bass we caught. We were amazed how many bass we might take from the same place without catching one that had been fin-clipped.

I learned fly casting by bass-bugging on the Charles. I figured out how to drive a bug under overhangs by letting my backcast straighten behind me and then throwing a firm narrow loop. I learned to read the targets and cast accurately. Bass, I understood, didn't like to move far to eat. If I dropped a bug two feet from a tree trunk or stump or the edge of the weeds, I got no strike. When I could land it three inches away, I'd let it sit and quiver for as long as I could stand it — which in those days wasn't very long. I'd give it a twitch ... pause ... then a harder jerk that would make the bug gurgle softly ... let the rings dissipate ... wait ... and no matter how intensely I anticipated it, I was always startled when the water imploded and the bug disappeared into the maw of a bass that had finally been tempted beyond resistance.

I found it just as exciting when Dad cast the bug as when I did.

When I dropped my backcast and slapped the water behind me, Dad gleefully splashed me with his paddle. That was as close as he ever came to giving me a fly-casting lesson. I always waited for him to hit the water with his backcast so I could return the favor — which I surely would have — but he never did. When I overshot into the bushes, and he had to paddle in so I could get unhooked, I would apologize for ruining a good spot. He'd feign disgust and grumble, "You'd make one terrific squirrel fisherman," but then he'd quickly say, "Hey, it's like golf—never up, never in. It's better to be long than short."

Dad never seemed to be either long or short, and I suppose I spent more time with the rod than he did. But we always caught an equal number of bass. The rules of our game pretty much guaranteed it.

As a boy, I loved playing three-strikes-and-out for Charles River largemouths more, even, than baseball. I loved the way the swallows and bats came out at dusk and the bullfrogs grumped and the bluegills spatted and the water grew black and glassy and mysterious. Dad and I respected the silence of it. Once the sun sank behind the hills, we talked little, and then in whispers, and when a big bass inhaled a bug, the *ka-chug!* seemed to echo across the water. I can still hear it.

When I was young, my family took summer vacations in the Machias Lakes region of northeastern Maine, a full day's drive from our home in eastern Massachusetts, as guests of our friends George and Marian Smith. I remember Uncle George as a bear of a man who chewed cigar stubs and whose intriguing gold incisor flashed when he grinned, which was most of the time. He had an endless supply of stories, which he told with an exaggerated Down East twang and more colorful language than my mother liked. He operated a string of sporting camps and guided salmon fishermen and deer hunters.

When he saw Mum and Dad and my sister and me loaded into one of his big lake canoes, Uncle George would shake his head and say, "How can a man fish with a wife and a hayrick full of small children?"

Sysladobsis Lake and Upper Dobsis and all the other interconnected lakes in the area had once been prime landlocked salmon water, and Dad had enjoyed marvelous fishing there. By the time we began visiting them as a family, however, the white perch and smallmouth bass had established themselves and the salmon fishing had deteriorated.

Family fishing was leisurely. Mum and Martha trolled and sunbathed. Dad and I cast streamers toward the rocky shoreline for bass and big Dardevle spoons into the shallow weedy coves for pickerel. Whenever we came upon a school of perch we tied on small streamers and did our best to fill the canoe with them. Butter-fried white perch fillets were delicious — although I think Dad secretly hoped to clean the salmon competitors out of the lake.

Once we dug some worms, anchored over a dropoff, and the four of us held a rod and dozed in the canoe. Mum, no slouch of a fisher-person, suddenly sat upright. "I've got a bite!" she screamed. An instant later Martha's rod dipped. "Me, too!" she squealed.

They set their hooks simultaneously and both of them were tied to large fish that took turns taking line from them. When they finally got their fish close to the canoe, Dad began laughing. He netted a single salmon of at least four pounds with two hooks in its mouth.

One summer we spent our vacation in Uncle George's cabin on Upper Dobsis. We had to drive over several rutted miles of abandoned logging road to get to the lake. The canoe was hidden in the bushes. We loaded it with our week's supplies, then paddled it across the lake to the one-room log cabin. A hand pump brought lake water to the sink. Kerosene lamps hung from wooden pegs. A one-hole outhouse stood out back.

After supper the first night, Dad said to me, "Let's go fishin'."

We paddled across the glassy lake in the gathering twilight. Somewhere a loon laughed in startling counterpoint to the quiet rhythm of our two paddles carving the water. The sky was pewter fading toward black, and already a few bright stars showed. Swallows ticked the lake's smooth surface with their wing tips.

I noticed a bright star moving sedately across the horizon. I pointed with my paddle. "What's that?" I said.

"Sputnik. That new Russian satellite."

Russian satellites, I thought, did not belong in the Maine sky.

"I remember a place," Dad whispered a moment later, "from a long time ago when I was here."

We nosed the canoe into a large cove. Scattered across its surface were the top halves of huge boulders — as large, some of them, as Volkswagen roofs. From his place in the stern Dad handed me a fly rod loaded with a deerhair bug. "Throw it against the rocks," he said. "Let's see what happens."

What happened was an hour of bass-bugging heaven. We counted the smallmouths we landed, although I forget the number now. Eight or ten, I would guess. None was smaller than three pounds. They lay against the boulders, and when they struck they exploded the mirrored surface of the cove. They fought like no Charles River largemouth I'd ever hooked — hard runs that zinged line off the reel, leaps that catapulted them several feet above the water.

We drifted in the cove, moving slowly on unfelt currents of air so that the paddler needed only to feather occasionally to keep the caster broadside to the next boulder target. We played three-strikes-and-out, and never were more than three or four casts necessary before the man with the rod found himself tied to a smallmouth.

We had only explored half of the cove when Dad said, "Let's quit."

"But —"

"We've got a whole week," he said quietly.

So we reeled in and paddled across the dark lake, following the wavering orange reflection of the kerosene lamp that Mum had set on a rock in front of the cabin.

I spent the next day in an impatient blur of anticipation. Come evening, we would revisit the magic cove. And we did, and the night was soft and the loons wailed and the swallows swooped and the bass were there. And they were there in undiminished numbers every night after that, too.

It was a Sure Thing.

Oddly, I found myself anticipating each evening with a little less eagerness as the days passed. Each successive night it seemed to me that those smallmouths crashed our bugs with just a shade less violence and jumped with less energy, and if we hadn't kept count, I would've believed that we caught fewer of them and that they were smaller.

In fact, however, our boulder-strewn cove gave us an hour of perfect smallmouth fishing every evening for the week our family stayed in Uncle George's log cabin on Upper Sysladobsis Lake in the Maine wilderness.

Dad and I recently talked about our week of twilights in the cove on Upper Dobsis. It was, we agreed, the best bass bugging either of us ever experienced, before then or since. "Paradise," said Dad.

"The stuff of fiction."

"A bona fide Sure Thing."

"I never told you this before," I said, "but after the first few nights, I found myself losing some of my enthusiasm for it."

"You, too?" he said.

"You?"

He smiled. "You seemed so eager. I didn't want to let you down."

"I was doing the same thing," I said. "I mean, you hauled us way up there into the Maine woods and you showed me this amazing fishing—how could I tell you it had stopped being so much fun?"

He nodded. "It *was* a slice of paradise, though, wasn't it?"

"Perfect," I agreed.

"Which," he said, "is the problem with paradise. It's just too darned perfect."

———

The decline of the smallmouth fishing in Winnipesaukee coincided (although I'm convinced it's not a coincidence) with the invention of bass boats and foot-operated electric motors and hi-tech spinning rigs and crankbaits and spinnerbaits and depth finders and all the other innovations that produced the boom of tournament bass fishing sometime in the 1980s. At first we noticed an occasional bass boat anchored in one of "our" coves.

Three men would be sitting up on their perches methodically tossing out spinning lures, and although we gave them wide berth, we noticed that they did seem to catch an awful lot of fish.

I fished Winnipesaukee twice last year with Dad. The first time we stayed out for two hours and landed three half-pound smallmouths. We guessed that a bass boat or two had already raked that shoreline.

The second time, a week later, we motored around the lake searching for a vacant cove. The bass boats were so heavily deployed that we never found a place to wet a line. That's when we began to reminisce about our long-ago week on Upper Dobsis. We agreed that we were ready for another shot at paradise. We figured that maybe we'd finally learned enough to appreciate it.

CHAPTER SEVEN

EX-PLORES AND EXPOTITIONS

*O*n a sweltering August afternoon thirteen summers ago, I said to my son, Mike (then nine), "Think you're man enough to lift one end of a canoe over your head?"

He pushed up the sleeve of his T-shirt and produced an admirable bicep.

I whistled appreciatively. "Then let's go fishin'," I said.

Mike and I had watched bluegills jiggle red-and-white bobbers many times, and he had trolled for Winnipesaukee smallmouths from his grandfather's canoe. The previous Christmas, Grampa had given Mike a Zebco spin-fishing outfit, a less-than-subtle reminder to Mike's Dad that perhaps the boy needed a little more encouragement. Mike quickly learned to whang a lure an admirable distance with his Zebco rig.

So far all of our shared fishing adventures had taken place either in other people's boats or from land, for the simple reason that my canoe was too heavy and cumbersome for one man to wrestle onto and off of my car by himself. It was a two-man job, and until now Mike did not qualify as one of them. But today, with the help of Mike's rocklike muscles, we would take our First Real Father-Son Fishing Trip.

For me, it was a Ceremonial Occasion. For Mike, I suspect it was nothing special. He liked fishing, and he had nothing better to do on this hot summer afternoon. Ceremonies are for adults.

Warner's Pond lay about a mile from the house. In the winter, the neigborhoods that cluster near its shores swarmed onto its ice to skate and build bonfires. I'd seen ice fishermen hunkered on it, and in the summer canoes and homemade rafts sometimes drifted on its surface. Adventuresome teenagers, I'd heard, sometimes camped out on the island. A suburban road nearly touched its eastern banks, and an eight-lane highway paralleled its shore on the north. A couple of times I had driven the dirt roadway to the sand beach to study it. Its edges were too weed-clogged for bobber-fishing or Zebco-casting from shore, but I had heard that it was full of panfish and largemouths and pickerel, and every spring the boys at the gas station whispered to me the secret news that someone had taken a big trout from Warner's. It was one of those places that I had always intended to investigate, but whenever the urge to go fishing had struck, I had opted for more distant waters.

Warner's seemed like the perfect place for this ceremony. I liked the idea of discovering something new with Mike, rather than showing him something already familiar to me.

When we were ready to launch the canoe, Mike insisted on taking the paddle. I understood that he did not intend a gesture of equal partnership. He had just never paddled a canoe and thought it looked like fun. Adventures in partnership would follow soon enough, I figured. So he weaved erratically around the pond, while I flycast a bluegill popper from the bow. I quickly discovered that the place was, indeed, full of panfish. The bluegills ran consistently large, and I caught a few crappies and small bass.

The hum and honk of traffic from the highway that paralleled the north shore mingled with birdcalls, insect buzzes, and bullfrog grumbles. Suburban backyards sloped down to the pond. There was one other craft on the water — a rubber raft that drifted aimlessly in the weeds near shore. Two pairs of bare legs protruded from it.

Mike paddled, I cast, and after a while it was easy to ignore the push of civilization around the edges of the pond. The sun blazed down, and Mike peeled off his T-shirt.

Once a bulge materialized under the lily pads, became a lazy wake, accelerated, charged the popper like a torpedo, and sliced my leader clean.

"What was *that*?" whispered Mike.

"Small pickerel."

"Wow!"

I waited for him to ask for his turn. He didn't. I kept casting and catching fish. He struggled bravely with the paddle. I considered instructing him on proper technique, sermonizing, perhaps, on the efficiency of the J-stroke, but decided that he was bright enough to figure it out by trial and error or to ask. Trial and error — and last-resort asking — had taught me many things, and I certainly didn't want to discourage Mike with oblique criticism.

Finally I said, "You want to catch a fish?"

"That's all right," he said. "I'm having fun."

"You like paddling?"

"It's okay. I think I'm getting the hang of it."

"You like watching me catch fish?"

"Sure."

"Well," I said, "I like paddling, too, and I'd like to watch you catch fish. So how about we swap?"

He nodded. "I guess it's your turn."

We converted Mike's end into the bow by rotating in our seats. He picked up his Zebco and whanged a Mepps spinner out there, and it didn't take more than two or three casts for him to hook a bluegill. His grin showed me that he enjoyed fishing almost as much as paddling.

I followed the shoreline until we came upon a shallow weed-choked cove. I noticed that a narrow meandering channel of open water cut through the weeds. I paddled into that channel and detected just the hint of current. I dipped my fingers into the water. It felt at least ten degrees cooler than the rest of the pond.

"Hey," I said to Mike. "How about an ex-plore?"

"A what?"

"An ex-plore. Your grandfather has always been very big on ex-plores. It's time you and I had one."

———

After dinner, and before he trudged down to his basement office for his evening of invisible writing, Dad made a ceremony of reading to me and my sister. Martha would crawl up onto his lap and I would sit cross-legged on the floor beside his chair. He usually selected a Winnie-the-Pooh story. Dad had special voices for each of the characters. His — and our — favorite was Eeyore, the melancholy donkey, whose life-is-stern-and-earnest philosophy especially appealed to Dad, I suspect.

Pooh and Christopher Robin, along with Eeyore and Rabbit and all of Rabbit's friends and relations and Tigger and Kanga and baby Roo (I can still hear Dad's voice for each of them — the television versions simply don't ring true to my ears, except for the animated Eeyore, whose voice could have been Dad's) often took what they called little "ex-plores" and more elaborate "expotitions" to mysterious corners of the Hundred-Acre Woods.

Ex-plores are spontaneous adventures, however small, and children (of all ages) cannot resist them. Whenever Dad and I were out on the water, he loved to announce an ex-plore. He would push the canoe deep into a previously un-ex-plored cove or up a feeder stream. Sometimes we flushed herons or ducks or geese. Sometimes we found muskrat houses. Sometimes we found pickerel or bass. Sometimes we found nothing at all. It didn't really matter whether we found anything. We understood that if every ex-plore produced an adventure, the adventures would begin to lose their appeal.

Dad had either the wisdom or the instinct to understand that kids — or at least I — had low tolerance for "lessons" but an insatiable appetite for adventures. The success of a fishing trip depended less on the number of fish we caught than on the quality of the adventure. Dad and I didn't always catch a lot of fish, but we always had fun.

When my kids began to get old enough to hold a rod and I found myself impatient with their fumbling, I asked Dad about his determinedly laissez-faire approach to fishing education. He had never given me lessons. He let me wallow around in my own bumbling. Somehow, I ended up addicted.

He shrugged. "What's your goal?" he asked.

"I want my kids to like fishing."

"Or do you want to show off their precocious fly-casting skills to your friends?"

"Nope," I said. "I just want them to know how much fun fishing is. I want to share it with them."

"Oh, they already like fishing," he said. "Everybody likes fishing, if they're given the chance. Unless, that is, some adult comes along to spoil it. You want your kids to like fishing, just don't get in the way. Take 'em out and follow their lead. They want to catch frogs? Take off your shoes and go catch some frogs with them. They get tired of it after a while? Do something else. Don't push. Fishing is just naturally fun. A love of fishing's in our human genes. Hunting, too — it's all in the same gene, I think — and if you can just leave it alone, it'll always be there. Better yet, nurture it." He smiled. "Remember, there's more to fishing than trying to catch fish. Skipping flat stones is fishing, too, right?"

I nodded. I remembered the day when we beached the canoe on a Maine lake to stretch our legs after a long and fishless morning of trolling streamers for landlocked salmon. Dad casually picked up a stone and flipped it sidearm across the surface of the lake. The stone skipped six or seven times before it sank to the bottom. He did it again, and got even more skips. "Can you do that?" he said.

I tried imitating him, and after several attempts I managed to produce a couple of skips. He repeated his performance. It became a contest that he kept winning, although I had a strong pitching arm. I studied his technique, tried, erred, revised my methods, and after a while my stones were skipping six or seven times across the water. I figured out that successful flat-stone-skipping was a complex art. It depended on careful stone selection (flat-sided, neither too small nor too heavy), proper grip (forefinger curled around the edge), and arm motion (elbow cocked in against the hip, quick wristy sidearm flip with the flat edge of the stone parallel to the water's surface).

Flat-stone skipping was a fishing adventure — a kind of explore. Dad and I still use it as our metaphor for the infinitely varied ways a father can share time in the outdoors with one of his children. I have challenged each of my kids to flat-stone-skipping contests. All three of them have become deft skippers and enthusiastic ex-plorers. Flat-stone skipping, all three generations agree, is fishing, too.

Dad and I dug worms from our vegetable garden. We rolled up our pantslegs and hand-captured crawfish from Walden Pond. We turned over planks in abandoned lumber yards and pounced on the fat crickets we found hiding underneath. We waded in rocky streams, and one of us would hold a landing net while the other rolled over upstream rocks to loosen hellgrammites. We turned on the lawn sprinkler at dusk, and a couple hours later we teamed up to pick nightcrawlers by flashlight. We baited minnow traps with bread and oatmeal. We caught yellow perch and sliced strips from their bellies to make skittering baits for pickerel.

Gathering bait was always an ex-plore — as often as not more productive and fun than catching fish with it.

We dug for Indian artifacts after lunch on the island in Fairhaven Bay. We abandoned beaten paths to follow brooks up toward their origins in swamps. When we hunted grouse and woodcock in New Hampshire, we drove unfamiliar dirt roads and never hesitated to stop at a new spot that looked as if it might hold a bird.

Ex-plores were spur-of-the-moment responses to some immediate stimulus. If we needed bait, we caught some. If we saw an intriguing cove or alder run, we investigated it. If there were flat stones lying on the shore, we skipped them.

Expotitions, on the other hand, were adventures that we planned and plotted with the care and anticipation of a major military maneuver. We spread topographic maps over our kitchen table and read woodcock runs and trout ponds from their legends. Then we slogged through swamp or push-poled our canoe into places where, as Dad liked to say, the hand of man had never set foot. Or so we liked to believe.

We organized expotitions to distant storied places, often in the company of Dad's friends. Bob Elliot organized an expotition to a few of Maine's lesser-known Atlantic salmon rivers — the Machias, the Dennys, the Narraguagus. We raised no fish in a week (the runs were just beginning to come back in those years), but I saw a few of those magnificent endangered gamefish being trapped and moved over the dams. We hunted grouse in Corey Ford's Field and Stream cover near Hanover, New Hampshire. I caught a twenty-inch brown trout on a Light Cahill (the memory remains crystal clear thirty-five years later — it was my first big trout) from a pool that Baird Hall showed us on northern Vermont's Lamoille River. Harold Blaisdell led expotitions to Furnace Brook and Otter Creek and Lake Champlain, and to the White and the Battenkill rivers, in his part of Vermont.

We trolled for landlocked salmon in Sebago and Moosehead Lakes. We anchored over points and dropoffs and dangled crawfish and crickets in just about every deepwater smallmouth lake in New Hampshire. One August we trekked to the uppermost waters of the Connecticut River near the Canadian border, where I tried ... and erred ... and eventually figured out how to fish a spinner fall for rainbow trout in the dark.

I've taken my kids on some expotitions. We spent a week rafting the Middle Fork of the Salmon River in the Frank Church River of No Return Wilderness in Idaho. We slept under the stars and fly-fished for native cutthroats. Sarah, who was then eight, liked to strip in the little gemlike trout I hooked. She kept count of them, and when we made camp in the evening she took my fly rod down to the river and tried to imitate my casting. For the most part, I bit my tongue and let her try and err, and she got so she could slop out a dry fly twenty feet or so.

On the fourth evening an eight-inch cutt flashed up and gobbled the fly. She lifted the rod instinctively and caught her first dry-fly trout all by herself. I was glad that I was sitting back on the rocks watching instead of standing by her elbow whispering instructions. It was too dark to record the event on film. But the picture of her big brown-eyed grin remains clear in my memory.

Mike, Melissa, Sarah, and I spent a day in Ben Trebken's *Amethyst* five hours out to sea where the horizon completely encircled us. We caught albacore and yellowfin and skipjack tuna, and when one of *Amethyst's* engines quit on the way to port, we limped in under the stars. In recent years we've spent our Memorial Day weekends at Blaine Moore's summer house on an island in Maine's Great Pond—a more civilized version of my boyhood weeks at Sysladobsis and Upper Dobsis. We have yet to find a magic cove on Great Pond, but Sarah has caught smallmouths on Woolly Buggers she tied herself.

My kids love expotitions. But I think they prefer the spontaneity of ex-plores, just as Dad and I did.

———•◦•———

Without the tell-tale channel of open water cutting through the weeds, the inlet to Warner's Pond would have been nearly impossible to discover. It snuck in at a sharp angle through a curtain of thick pond-side foliage. Mike, up in the bow, had to push aside the trailing willow branches as we nosed the canoe into it.

We abruptly found ourselves in a wild woody tunnel. Foliage arched overhead, blocking out the sun. Redwing blackbirds and cedar waxwings flitted among the alder and blackberry that clogged the margins of the brook. Wild grapevines twined around the trees.

After a few minutes, I noticed that I couldn't hear any traffic noises or see any suburban houses, and it was easy to fool myself into believing that Mike and I had entered a kind of magical wilderness island in the middle of suburbia.

Mike tried to make a few casts, but the brush grew too thick and the brook was too narrow and twisted for his level of Zebco accuracy. So he laid his rod on the bottom of the canoe and leaned forward in his seat.

I paddled us slowly through this dark natural tunnel. Painted turtles slipped off logs into the water. A black duck with half a dozen little ones strung out behind her disappeared under some trailing branches. We jumped a wood duck. A muskrat angled across the brook ahead of us, then abruptly dived. Here and there a bluegill spatted.

The brook forked, and I chose the more navigable of the two options. As I pushed up into it, it widened and became shallower, opening here and there into pools where we paused to make a few casts. Mike caught a couple of bluegills.

Then it narrowed so tight that Mike had to pull on the bushes to get us through. Then it opened up again into a slow-moving slough. It looked like marvelous bass water — fallen trees, steep banks, an irregular brushlined shoreline, patches of lily pads. Mike made a few casts and caught another bluegill.

We continued upstream, and although I knew better, I could almost believe that Mike and I were original explorers.

The foliage thinned out, and then the brook was winding through a marsh. The grass grew six feet tall along the sides. It looked like trout water.

Finally the canoe scraped, then ground to a stop on a gravel riffle. We had come, I estimated, two or three miles.

"End of the line, I guess," I said to Mike, and as I spoke, I realized that we had not exchanged a word since we entered the brook.

"We can drag it up and go farther," he said.

"Let's save that for another day."

He nodded. It was good to have new ex-plores waiting for us.

We swapped ends and I paddled us downstream. Mike fished steadily. He seemed to get the feel for short accurate casting toward likely targets. He caught a small pickerel, several bluegills, a yellow perch. When we returned to the slough, I expected him to nail a bass, but he didn't.

He cast directly ahead of the boat to the place where the brook narrowed and quickened. Suddenly he grunted. His rod arched.

"What've you got?" I said.

"I don't know." There was an edge of panicky excitement in his voice. "Something big."

"Keep your rod high," I said, in spite of all my training in trial-and-error learning theory. "Don't try to horse him in."

Mike worked the fish close to the canoe. Then it flashed near the surface. "It's a trout," I said. "You've got yourself a trout. Your first trout."

He grabbed the leader and hoisted it aboard. It was a rainbow of thirteen or fourteen inches, as silvery and fat as a fresh sea-run steelhead. It flopped once in the bottom of the canoe and threw the Mepps spinner.

Mike picked up the fish. "Shall we put him back?" he said.

"It's your fish."

"I'm gonna put him back."

He leaned over the side and let the trout slide into the water. Then he straightened up, wiped his hands on his pants, and turned to me. "Grampa likes ex-plores, huh?"

I nodded.

"Too bad he couldn't be here."

"He would've liked this one a lot," I said.

CHAPTER EIGHT

INTO THE WOODS

I was born on the eve of World War II. I was little more than a toddler when Dad made me a wooden rifle and taught me the manual of arms. "A gun," he said, "is a weapon. It kills things. It must be treated respectfully. Even a wooden one."

Later, when I began to acquire a boy's arsenal of cap guns, Dad told me, "Never—*ever*—point a gun—*any* gun, even a toy—at somebody else."

Then came the magical Christmas when I found a Daisy air rifle under the tree. I caught Dad staring thoughtfully at me as I stroked its barrel, and I nodded to him. "I know," I said.

"You could put out somebody's eye."

"Yes. I know."

"If I ever find out—"

"Don't worry."

We took the heavy single-shot .22 target rifle into the woods behind the house and shot tin cans and paper targets. Dad showed me how to shoot from the prone position, and sitting and kneeling and off-hand. I learned how to wrap the sling around my left arm, squint one-eyed through the peep-sight, take a breath, let half of it out, and squeeze—never jerk—the trigger.

But the real point of the lessons was not lost on me. Safety, I knew, was more important than accuracy. A .22 bullet could travel a mile through the air. It made an impressive hole in a tin can. Never load a gun until you're ready to shoot it. And whether it's loaded or not, always know where your muzzle is pointed. Always point it away from people.

Once when I was very young Dad took me into the woods, slipped a shell into his shotgun, and handed it to me. "Shoot that," he said, pointing to a rusty oil drum fifteen or twenty yards away.

"How can I miss?" I said.

"Just shoot it."

The shotgun felt heavy and outsized, and the barrel wavered across the target. "Press it firmly against your shoulder," said Dad. "Just like the .22."

I steadied the gun and squeezed the trigger. Nothing happened.

"That thing by your thumb," he said. "It's the safety. When you're ready to shoot, you push it up."

I did. Then I aimed and shot. The oil drum collapsed in an explosion of rust.

"Wow!" I said.

Dad said nothing. He had made his point.

———

I was Dad's fishing partner for many years before I ever went hunting. There was an element to hunting that was missing from fishing, and I understood it: Treat a fly rod heedlessly and it might break; mishandle a gun and somebody could die.

Fishing was for boys, or boys and men together.

Hunting was for men who trusted their lives to each other.

My time, I figured, would come.

So I waited. On October Saturdays I got up early so I could take Dad's cased shotgun from the basement gun cabinet and prop it near the back door beside the picnic basket, Dad's boots, and the canvas bag that held shells, Milkbones, spare bells, dry socks, and dog collars. When Grampa Grouse, his partner, arrived, I ate bacon and eggs with the men while the dogs whimpered and whined under the table. And when they returned on Sunday evenings I met them at the car to count the grouse they had brought home and help lug the gear inside.

Dad showed me how to clean his shotgun, and that became my job. After a successful weekend, I helped him clean the birds, too. Cleaning birds was not that different from cleaning fish.

In November Dad hunted deer in Maine. In December he arose in the dark to go for ducks.

In the cool of August and September evenings, Dad and Bing, our Brittany, held their bird-hunting version of spring training. They visited the local farms, secured permission of the landowners, and criss-crossed the fields and hedgerows for newly fledged pheasants. Dad's weapon was a loud police whistle with which he attempted to remind Bing of his proper behavior.

I generally went along. The mix of goldenrod and ragweed stood nearly head-high on me and invariably gave me a vile dose of hayfever, but I didn't mind. This was hunting, and I was one of the hunters. When Bing pointed, Dad would grab his check cord and creep up behind him, whispering endearments and reminding him to hold steady. My job was to move ahead of the point and flush the birds and then try to mark them down so we could follow up the singles.

I had read plenty about southern quail hunting. Northern immature-pheasant hunting was identical except for the fact that we didn't carry guns, which seemed like an insignificant difference. The birds were small and brown and they exploded from the ground in coveys of six or eight and flew swiftly. To me, it was hunting, and so what if I ended up with watery eyes and runny nose.

But when October came around, I stayed home.

While I waited, I stalked milkweed pods and toadstools and dragonflies with my BB gun and remembered how that oil drum had disintegrated. I lost interest in hunting down my playmates with cap pistols. The gun games we played weren't that much fun, because I had promised not to aim directly at the neighborhood soldiers, Indians, and crooks. One day, I knew, I'd hunt real game with real guns.

I figured that when that day came, it would be accompanied by solemn ceremony. I sensed, although I could not articulate, that my first hunting trip would mark a significant rite of passage from boyhood into the world of men, like my first drink of whiskey, my first drag on a cigar, my first sexual encounter.

A nor'easter blew in on Friday, driving before it sheets of hard rain that ripped the yellow leaves from the maples behind our suburban Massachusetts house. On Saturday morning the wind had subsided, but the rain continued hard, steady, and cold. Dad held a long and mournful phone conversation with Grampa Grouse, then announced that it looked like no hunting this weekend. He made a pass at assembling the week's trash for a trip to the dump. He went down into the cellar and examined the stack of storm windows that would soon need to be hung. He drove downtown to the hardware store and returned an hour later, empty-handed.

Around noon he appeared in the kitchen clad in foul-weather gear and lugging his Winchester Model 21. Bing scrambled from beneath the kitchen table and began to prod the back door with his nose, whining and whimpering.

"You're going hunting, aren't you?" said Mum.

"Yep."

"Oh, brother," she said, failing to hide a smile.

"Want to come?" said Dad to me.

"It's raining."

"Sure. Coming?"

"You bet," I said.

We drove to Lincoln, not ten minutes from our house. A road now cuts through the pine grove near where we parked that day, and a pod of cedar-sheathed contemporary homes presently snuggles into the hillside where we hunted. But forty-odd years ago it was just a big field head-high in popple and birch. I tracked behind Dad as well as my ten-year-old legs would permit. The hard rain clattered on the hood of my oilskin slicker. My legs and feet were soaked in an instant. Head down, I trudged after him, intent on keeping up.

Suddenly he stopped. "Point," he hissed.

Bing was stretched out, motionless, his head curved awkwardly sideways. My father walked past him. I heard an odd whistle, glimpsed a brown ball of feathers rising from the ground, saw Dad's shotgun move to his shoulder, noted the way the raindrops bounced off the barrels, heard a single report, and watched the bird plummet to the ground. Bing bounded forward and returned an instant later with a dead bird in his mouth.

Dad said, "Good dog," and took it from him. Then he turned and handed the bird to me.

I held it in both hands. It weighed less than I expected. It was about half the size of the grouse I had helped Dad clean. It seemed frail, mostly feathers. I smoothed them with my fingertip. Two boggled eyes were perched oddly at the top of his head. He had a long, narrow beak. He looked, I thought, more like an insect than a bird.

"It's a woodcock," said Dad quietly. "A lovely little bird. The beak is for catching worms underground. They can move it around even after it's in the earth. The eyes are placed up there so he can look around when his beak is in the ground. His ears are in front of his eyes and his brain is upside down."

I handed the little bird back to him. He hefted it gently in the palm of one hand for a moment before thrusting it into his game pocket. "It's a shame to shoot them," he said. "Wish we could put them back, like trout."

Three more times that afternoon Bing pointed. Three more times Dad's twenty-gauge barked. Three more times Bing trotted in with a dead woodcock in his mouth. "Well, that's a limit," said Dad. He broke his shotgun and we cut back to the car.

Four shots in an hour. One limit of woodcock. It seemed like a very simple sport.

The rain ended that night. Sun drenched the autumn woods on Sunday. Hunting is illegal on Sundays in Massachusetts, but on

Monday Dad unexpectedly came home early from work. "Want to go hunting?" he said to me.

"Yes, sir!"

We drove back to Lincoln, parked in the same place, and trekked to the birch and popple hillside. And that afternoon I learned my first truth about woodcock. We hunted for two hours. We flushed nothing.

"You must've shot them all," I said to Dad afterward.

"Doubt it," he said.

"Then where were all the woodcock?"

He shrugged, and when he gave me his answer, it was as if he were equating the mysterious comings and goings of woodcock with good fortune, or life itself. "They migrate," he said.

After that rainy woodcock adventure, I spent another two years watching Dad and Grampa Grouse head for New Hampshire on Saturday mornings in the fall and return on Sunday evenings. I continued to refrain from being heard, because I knew Dad already understood that I wanted to go along. But I made a point of being seen, just to be sure he wouldn't forget me. I waited with as much patience as I could muster for my chance.

One Friday evening in October I noticed that he and Mum were whispering in the kitchen. Then he called me in. "Grampa Grouse is sick," he said to me. "You want to come along this weekend?"

"Hunting, you mean?"

"Yep."

This invitation fell far short of the solemn ceremony I had

expected would accompany the occasion of my first full-fledged weekend grouse-hunting excursion to New Hampshire, but I took my cue from Dad. "Well," I said, "sure. I guess so."

"Good. Set your alarm."

During the two-hour drive to New Hampshire, Dad explained that "corning along" did not mean I would carry a gun in the woods. "You'll walk behind me. Always stay behind me. You've got to keep up. If you can't keep up, you'll have to wait in the car. When we flush a bird, go to the ground. Understand?"

I nodded.

"Grouse," he said, "flush suddenly. We'd like the dog to point them, but he rarely does. Grouse are too nervous. So they usually surprise us. They fly fast, and you can never predict what direction they'll go in. I've got to know exactly where you are all the time. When a bird flies, you'd better be flat on the ground."

"I understand," I said.

We left the highway, and soon we were rolling over country roads past woodlands and meadows and dairy farms. The hills glowed in their autumn colors. Dad pulled into an overgrown dirt roadway. "First Chance Cover," he announced.

He uncased his shotgun while Bing squirted the bushes.

"Okay," said Dad. "Stay close." He called the same thing to Bing. "Close, boy."

Five minutes into the woods, I heard a sudden explosion. Dad yelled, "Mark!" A moment later he turned to me. "I told you to drop to the ground."

"Why?"

"That was a grouse."

"I didn't know."

"You've got to go to the ground. I don't want to shoot you."

"Okay."

"Don't wait to see the bird. When you hear him, or when I yell, you go down. Got it?"

"Yes, sir."

A little farther along when I heard that startling *Brrrt!* of wings, I threw myself to the ground. Dad yelled "Mark!" and his shotgun roared almost simultaneously. And then he called, "Fetch, Bing. Dead bird."

With my face pressed to the ground, I missed it all. I stood up in time to see Bing prancing to Dad with a grouse in his mouth. Dad knelt and the dog dropped the bird into his hand. Dad patted Bing's muzzle. "Good work, boy," he murmured. He stroked the bird's feathers, then tucked it into his game pocket. He turned to me. "That's what we're after," he said. "That's what it's all about. What'd you think?"

"Good shot."

"Yeah?"

I shrugged. "Actually, I didn't see anything. I was lying on the ground."

He grinned. "Good."

"But I bet it was a good shot."

"It was," he said. "Every time you hit a flying grouse it's a good shot."

In spite of my youthful energy and enthusiasm, I had to struggle to keep pace with Dad, who moved through the woods with swift efficiency and never seemed to tire. Juniper tangles caught my feet and muck sucked at my boots and birch whips snapped against my face and briars scratched the backs of my hands. But I was determined to keep up without complaining. I might be too young to carry a gun, but I was not too young to go hunting, and I was old enough not to complain. I understood that I had an apprenticeship to serve. I had to serve it honorably.

Grouse hunting, I learned, entailed a high ratio of tough miles walked to birds moved, and when it happened, it happened so suddenly that if I was lagging too far back I missed it all. It was not a laid-back sport like fishing from a canoe. There were no aimless ex-plores, no bait-catching or flat-stone skipping, no loafing. In the woods with guns, Dad and I were not equal partners. I was the apprentice. He was the boss. I did as I was told.

We hunted hard and purposefully all morning. At noon we sat against a sun-warmed stone wall by a little spring-fed brook and ate the lunches Mum had packed for us—woodsie sandwiches (corned beef, American cheese, and mayonnaise) and homemade applesauce cake. I took my first slug of coffee from the thermos—a small but significant ceremonial occasion all by itself. When we finished, Dad abruptly stood and said, "Can't sit too long. Dogs and men'll get all bogged down and stiff-legged."

The afternoon turned gray and chilly. My boots grew heavy. I stumbled and slogged through the thickets, struggling, now, to keep up. Dad plowed on, as energized as he had been back in First Chance. Now and then a grouse flew, and Dad shot at some of them. I learned that getting a fair shot at a flying grouse defined a successful hunt. Hitting one was a rare and wonderful achievement, even for a skilled and experienced hunter.

By the time we quit I was exhausted. Bing and Dad both seemed disappointed that we had run out of daylight.

We drove over to the Valley Hotel in Hillsboro. The dining room was full of middle-aged men wearing faded canvas pants and frayed flannel shirts and gray stubble on their chins. Setters and pointers and spaniels dozed in a tangle among the men's feet under the tables. They talked about thornapple and grape and alder, No. 8 shot and modified chokes, over-and-unders and side-by-sides, flushing dogs and pointing dogs and hunting grouse with no dogs. Now and then a hunk of beef accidentally fell under the table. I practiced being seen and not heard.

After dinner Dad took me to the little movie house where we saw — honest — *The Man with the Atomic Brain*. It was, I recall, a terrific film. But I dozed through the last half of it.

I had pancakes and bacon and my own cup of coffee for breakfast despite Dad's warning that pancakes would bog me down.

It was a crisp October Sunday morning. The narrow dirt roads wound under gold and crimson canopies of beech and maple. The goldenrod in the fields glittered with melted frost.

We stepped into the day's first cover. I was still trying to get un-bogged-down and keep pace with Dad when he suddenly hissed, "C'mere. Quick."

I hurried up to him. He pointed. "Look."

Bing stood beneath an apple tree, gazing intently upward into its bare branches. A grouse sat there looking down at him. Dad pressed his shotgun into my hands. "Take him," he said.

I hefted the gun. "Is it loaded?"

"Hurry. It'll fly. Of course it's loaded."

I lifted the shotgun to my shoulder and sighted over the wavering barrel. The grouse craned its neck.

I pressed the trigger.

"The safety," whispered Dad. "Quick."

I remembered I had only fired a shotgun once in my life. It had obliterated a rusty oil drum. I pushed the safety forward, took a deep breath, exhaled half of it, tried to steady the front sight on the nervous grouse, and pulled the trigger. I don't recall seeing the bird fall. I probably flinched and closed my eyes. But I did hear Dad shout, "Yeah! You got him. Great shot!"

A moment later Bing trotted in with my bird in his mouth. Dad took it from him, smoothed its feathers, and handed it to me. "Your first grouse," he said. "You have been bloodied. Congratulations."

He held his hand to me and I shook it. It was our first man-to-man handshake.

I carried that grouse by its feet through the rest of the cover. My legs remained light and springy all day, and I had no trouble keeping up with Dad.

———

After that, I followed Dad through grouse covers many times, and although I did not carry a gun and was still serving my apprenticeship, I realized that I had become his hunting partner, too. I learned to drop to one knee when a bird flushed so I could see it all. I noticed how Dad moved through the thickest cover with his gun always at ready, and how quickly everything happened when a bird flew. I watched the way he approached thick corners and field edges, how he and Bing worked as a team. I noticed the kinds of places from which grouse tended to flush, and how they flew, and where a man with a gun should be standing when it happened in order to have a fair shot.

I also noticed that the muzzle of his shotgun never pointed in my direction.

Now and then a young and foolish bird hopped onto a stone wall or fluttered up into a tree instead of bursting away, and then Dad would hand me the gun and I would shoot it.

"There's not much to shooting a sitting grouse," I said to him once.

"Grouse are wily birds," he answered. "It takes a good hunter to get that close to one. Lots of hunters shoot them on the ground. Men who hunt them without dogs, that's what they try to do. Nothing to be ashamed of."

I wasn't exactly ashamed. But I noticed that Dad only shot at flying grouse.

I followed in Dad's footsteps for two seasons, and it was just before the third when he decided that I was ready for my first shotgun. It was a single-barrel, one-shot twenty-gauge Savage. "I know," he said when he gave it to me. "You were probably hoping for a fancy double like mine. A man's gun, right?"

I shrugged. I was thrilled to have my own gun and to know that I'd be allowed to carry it in the woods. But he was right. A single-shot did seem like a kid's gun. I had already developed a fondness for the sleek side-by-side doubles Dad and his companions all carried.

"Well, listen," he said, reading my mind as he could do so well. "This is *not* a kid's gun. *No* gun is a kid's gun. This shoots real shotgun shells and you can kill things with it. Understand?"

I nodded.

"See, it's got a thumb safety, just like doubles have. So when you do get your double, you'll be used to it. Grouse hunting, you've got to be quick. Pushing off the safety's got to be instinctive. The good thing about a thumb safety is that it automatically clicks on whenever you break the gun. That's a very good thing."

He certainly liked to harp on safety, I thought. But I understood.

"Having only one shot'll teach you to make your first one count. And always remember this: After you shoot, the first thing you do is break open your gun. Got it?"

"Yes, sir."

When we stepped into our first cover that season, we talked strategy. Instead of following behind Dad, I would, for the first time in my life, take my own route parallel to him. We would whistle and call to each other, he reminded me. We must always know where the other guy is, and never *ever* shoot in his direction. We would split an alder run where, he said, we might find a pod of flight woodcock. Duke, our new setter, would work between us. A grouse usually lived there, too. He tended to scurry ahead of the dog and flush from the field edge at the end of the thicket.

As I moved through the alders, I was acutely conscious of the fact that I had only taken one shot at a flying bird in my life. I had been trailing Dad through Harold Blaisdell's Vermont grouse covers the previous fall when we emerged on the high banks of a creek. Uncle Harold and his dog were far off to our right. We heard a yell. Dad peered up the creek, then quickly handed me his gun. "Get ready!" he said, pointing.

Flying down the middle of the river toward us was a single black duck.

"Shoot him," said Dad.

I didn't have time to think, or aim, or ponder the fact that I had never discharged a shotgun at a moving object of any kind. I took the gun, raised it to my shoulder, flicked off the safety, and shot the duck.

I had seen Dad miss plenty of flying grouse and woodcock in two years of trailing him through the woods. I knew wing-shooting wasn't easy. But on that first morning when I carried my own gun in the woods, I had never missed.

I nearly stepped on the woodcock. He twittered up from my feet and corkscrewed through the thick alders, zig-zagging and darting erratically. I raised my gun, tried to aim, pulled the trigger, remembered the safety, and thumbed it off. The woodcock was nearly out of range. I hastily shot in his direction. He fell to the ground.

From the other side of the cover, Dad called, "Get him?"

"Yep."

By the time Dad got to me, I was kneeling to take the wood-cock from Duke's mouth. I looked up and grinned. Dad was not smiling. He was frowning at my gun, which I had laid on the ground. "I told you," he said, "always break the gun after you shoot."

"Right. I'm sorry."

"What if that was the double you wanted?"

I understood. There would be a live shell in the second bar-rel. The safety was off. "It won't happen again," I said.

"I'll take the gun away if you can't treat it right."

"I know."

He stared at me for a moment, then smiled. "Okay," he said. "Good shooting. Let's hunt."

Fifty yards farther on Duke bumped a woodcock from in front of me. It rose to the alder tops, then slanted off to the right. My new shotgun came up to my shoulder, swung, and shot the bird. I never thought about it. It just happened.

I carefully broke open my gun and waited for Duke to retrieve. Dad called, "Well?"

"Got 'im," I yelled. "And I broke my gun open."

"Well, good," was all he said.

The two woodcock in my game pocket made a pleasantly hefty little weight against the small of my back. I was, I decided, a remarkably gifted wingshot. My new gun and I couldn't miss. In fact, I had never missed a shot at a flying bird in my life. Who needed two barrels, anyway?

We found our covers full of early woodcock flights that day, and the grouse were thick, too, and before it was over I had sent a box of shells, one at a time, through that single new barrel of mine. I never hit another feather.

CHAPTER NINE

FIELD AND STREAM GROUSE

*A*fter I got my own gun, I hunted with Dad whenever he went, which was every weekend of the season. I hit flying woodcock with remarkable regularity—not frequency, but with that same regularity I'd established my first day with my new single-barrel Savage.

I'd hit a couple, miss twenty or so, then hit another one.

My success with flying grouse was even more regular: I never hit a single one of them. Not one.

I missed easy shots and hard ones, straight-aways and crossers, in-comers and out-goers, high-fliers and grass-cutters, darters and zig-zaggers. I missed grouse that I kicked up, grouse that Duke pointed, grouse that burst out of trees, grouse that Dad flushed to me. I missed grouse that darted through pine trees and grouse that sailed across open fields. I shot fast, I shot slow. I tried to lead them, I snap-shot at them. It didn't matter. I missed them all.

If I hadn't dropped an occasional woodcock, I would've thought there was something wrong with my gun.

But the explanation was clear: I was a completely inept wingshot.

Dad just smiled and shrugged. "Hitting a flying grouse is the hardest thing to do in hunting," he said. "Every time somebody hits one he knows he's been lucky. There's nothing to be ashamed of, missing a grouse. The best grouse shot in the world misses way more than he hits.

"Yeah, well nobody misses *all* of them," I grumbled.

"Absolutely right," he said. "So you've just got to keep shooting. They'll start falling. The only rule I know about hitting grouse is you've got to shoot. The guys who bring home the most birds, they're generally the ones who get the most shots. Getting off a shot is the point of grouse hunting. You're good at that. You've got quick reflexes. Every time you send a charge of number eights in the direction of a flying grouse, you've got a chance to bring him down. See, you're actually a pretty good grouse hunter. Figure it out. At the end of a day, I bet you get off as many shots as anybody."

"I must be doing something wrong."

"Nope," he said. "I've watched you. Nothing wrong with your technique. Keep shooting. The old law of averages is bound to catch up with you. Then you'll probably knock down five in a row."

I loved hunting. I loved the New England countryside in the fall. I loved the teamwork of it, moving through the woods parallel to Dad, with Duke criss-crossing between us. I loved figuring out where a grouse might lie and how I might make him fly so Dad or I would get a shot, and I thrilled every time one flushed. I loved analyzing topographic maps and driving back roads and tracking down rumors in search of new covers. I loved our meandering conversations on the long rides to and from New

Hampshire and between covers. I loved Saturday nights at the Valley Hotel. I loved the democratic companionship of Dad's friends, who became mine after we'd hunted together, men like Burt Spiller and Harold Blaisdell, John Brennan and Corey Ford and Lee Wulff.

I loved shooting, and I never took a shot that I didn't think would hit the bird. I didn't even mind missing.

But I hated missing *every* grouse I shot at.

Dad and the others we hunted with missed often, I noticed. Sometimes they cursed the bird or the various natural or supernatural forces that caused them to miss. Sometimes they even cursed their own poor marksmanship, although these curses sounded mild and half-hearted coming from the mouths of men who had shot plenty of grouse and knew they would shoot plenty more.

Still, I realized that there was no shame in missing. The odds always favored the grouse.

I kept shooting, and I waited, with declining optimism, for the law of averages to kick in. It occurred to me that it was definitely possible for a man to go through his entire life without ever hitting a flying grouse, just by missing them one at a time. That's the flip side of the law of averages. A coin can come up tails a hundred times in a row.

Sometimes I believed I had literally been cursed, that the Fates had singled me out — me, precisely because I loved this sport and persevered so diligently at it — for their tragic malediction. Like Sisyphus, I shoved mightily at my boulder even as I grew to believe I would never roll it to the top of the mountain.

By the time I was sixteen I had become pretty good at hitting curve balls with a baseball bat and swishing jump shots and blasting out of sand traps. I won archery tournaments and footraces. But my excellent hand-eye coordination and athleticism and enthusiasm for hunting were no proof against the omnipotence of the Red Gods.

"Finding birds and getting shots at them," Dad kept telling me. "That's hunting. Hitting them is shooting. That's different. You're a very good hunter."

He didn't need to finish his thought: I was a very bad shooter.

I figured that if, just once, the Gods' attention was diverted, or if they took pity on me, and I was allowed to shoot one flying grouse, I could live with never doing it again. Until that happened, I felt I was still an apprentice grouse hunter. I did not belong among the bloodied men at the Valley Hotel on a Saturday night. For no matter how I looked at it, the ultimate point of grouse hunting was shooting them out of the air.

So I roamed the woods for all of that first season with my new Savage, and the next season as well, hunting hard, shooting often, dropping the odd unfortunate woodcock — and missing grouse with absolutely perfect regularity.

A few times a grouse flushed between Dad and me, and we both shot simultaneously, and the bird came down. Dad called them "doubles," and tried to give me credit for hitting them. I didn't argue. It was possible that I had, in fact, sent a pellet into one of those birds. It was even possible that I had hit it and Dad had missed.

I was grateful that he never tried to convince me that he had missed and that the bird should be credited entirely to me (although I had seen him do that with some of the men we hunted with). He knew that I wanted that first grouse — if it ever should happen — to be clean and unequivocal.

So I didn't count the "half-birds" of our doubles. As far as I was concerned, when it came to hitting flying grouse, I remained a virgin.

On a dark November Sunday afternoon toward the end of that second season we were pushing through some thick cover along the edge of a swamp. The woodcock had already passed through, and the grouse had been scarce in our covers that weekend. Snow spit down from the low gray sky. The taste of winter was in the air. It was the last hunt of the day before we would begin the long drive south to Massachusetts.

The grouse exploded from a pine thicket beside me, angled sharp left, then darted through a screen of evergreens. By the time I snapped off my shot, he had already disappeared.

"Git 'im?" yelled Dad as he always did.

"Nah." I often found myself wishing Dad wouldn't keep asking, because I was sick of always answering in the negative.

"Get a line on him?"

"I hardly saw him. Straight ahead, I'd say."

"Might as well follow him up."

A minute later Dad yelled to me. "Come over here."

When I got there he was kneeling on the ground. He extended his closed fist to me, then opened it. Two breast feathers lay in his palm. "I found these drifting in the air," he said. "I'd say we've got a bird down."

Dad hung his red hat from a bush. He called in Duke. "Dead bird," he told him. "Fetch."

Duke cocked his head. "You trying to tell me that *Bill* hit a grouse?" his expression seemed to say.

"Fetch," Dad repeated.

Duke seemed to shrug. He had proved to be too head-strong and wide-ranging to make a good grouse dog. He flushed more birds than he pointed, many of them out of range. Dad did a lot of yelling and whistle-blowing in the woods. But Duke was a superior retriever. He had an excellent nose, and he had often found birds that we didn't know had been hit.

He understood the command "Fetch." So he went snuffling around in his ever-widening circles. He burrowed under blow-down, investigated thickets, and we followed the sound of his bell as he moved out of sight. A wing-tipped grouse could run a long distance from where it had come down.

Dad and I kicked at fallen branches and clumps of brush. The snow began to fall thicker and darkness seeped into the woods.

Duke wandered back to us. "Wild goose chase," his expression said. "No bird down."

"Go on, fetch, dead bird," insisted Dad, and in the urgency of his tone I heard for the first time what he had until then succeeded in withholding from me: That he wanted me to shoot my first flying grouse as much as I wanted to.

So Duke half-heartedly went back to looking, and Dad and I continued to search, until finally I said, "Obviously I missed him."

Dad shook his head. "Sometimes they'll fly a long way with pellets in them. I hate to leave a dead bird out here for the foxes."

"Sometimes," I said, "you get feathers without hitting the bird."

He shrugged. "Sometimes that can happen."

"So what do we do?"

"Far as I'm concerned," said Dad, "you hit that grouse."

"Far as *I'm* concerned, I missed him."

He looked at me for a moment, then nodded. We never liked the idea of leaving a wounded bird in the woods. We'd look for an hour or more for a bird that we thought had been hit, and if we had to quit, it left a sour taste in our mouths for the rest of the day.

But to leave my first wing-shot grouse wounded in the woods was unthinkable. Now it was too dark to keep looking. We had no choice. We had to quit.

"Guess you must've missed him," said Dad finally. "If he was down, Duke would've found him."

———

I began to hit woodcock with somewhat greater frequency during my third season with my Savage. But the grouse curse continued.

Dad and I hunted most Saturdays with Burt Spiller in his covers around Rochester, both in New Hampshire and over the border in Maine. Burt was seventy and could not take the thick routes where the birds hid anymore. He wore a hearing aid, which enabled him to converse with someone who spoke loudly and to hear the flush of a nearby grouse, although the hearing aid did not help him locate direction. He was forced to take the field edges and woods roads and hope for an occasional passing shot at a grouse or woodcock. If we flushed a bird in Burt's direction, we would scream, "Mark! Burt! Your way." I know he failed to see a great many birds that flew right in front of him. He might not have heard our screams, or if he did, he didn't know where to look.

So while Dad and I kicked up birds and shot at most of them, whole days sometimes passed when Burt never dirtied his gunbarrels.

He never complained. He loved to be in the woods. And when he did shoot, he rarely missed.

If he noticed my unblemished perfection at missing flying grouse, he never mentioned it.

Once he and I were following a pair of overgrown ruts out of our Tripwire cover. It was a sun-drenched New England morning in early October. The beech leaves had not yet fallen from the trees that arched over the old roadway, so that we seemed to be strolling through a golden tunnel. Our guns hung at our sides, because the hunt was over. Dad and Duke were somewhere off to our left, returning to the car by their own route.

Suddenly Dad yelled, "Mark! Grouse! Your way!"

Burt heard Dad's voice, although I'm not sure he even knew that Dad was to our left. I was a step or two behind him, so I saw it all happen. Burt's little Parker twenty-gauge came up to port arms. His head swiveled from side to side. Then a grouse sliced silently through the screen of beeches and angled across the narrow roadway.

It didn't make it. In a motion too quick for my eye to follow, Burt's gun came to his shoulder, swung on the bird, and shot. The grouse crumpled in a burst of feathers. It was one of the most incredible shots I have ever seen — lightning fast, oily smooth, and deadly accurate, and that is essentially what I said to Burt.

He just shrugged. "I'm sorry," he said. I should've let you take him."

———

Dad and I hunted the last weekend of that bird season around Hanover, New Hampshire, as guests of Corey Ford and his marvelous old setter, Cider, who got his name because he "worked in the fall." Dan Holland, the hunting writer, and Hugh Grey, then editor of *Field & Stream*, were also with us.

I diligently practiced being seen and not heard that weekend and was rewarded with wide-ranging tales of famous men and places and memorable hunts.

The grouse also practiced being neither seen nor heard. All day Saturday we heard two wild flushes and saw nary a feather.

Sunday gave us less of the same. It was one of those chilly gray New England November days, closer to winter than fall. We drove from cover to cover and tended to linger longer in the warmth of the car as the day wound down, compensating with good companionship for the poor hunting.

Nobody had taken a single shot all weekend which, I realized, made me just as good a wingshot as the rest of them. I would rather we'd found a lot of birds. But at least my dismal marksmanship hadn't been exposed.

Sometime in the middle of the afternoon, Dad said, "I think we'll head home. We've got a long drive facing us."

"You can't go yet," said Corey. "We haven't hunted the Field and Stream cover. It's where we always finish up. I've been saving it."

Dad shrugged. He was too polite to point out that Corey's covers had all been consistently unproductive, and there was no reason to believe that this one would be any different.

So the five of us piled out of the wagon and walked down the long sloping woods-path, heading for the abandoned farm yard where Corey said the birdy part of the cover began. Cider snuffled along ahead of us, hunting diligently, as he had all weekend, in spite of the absence of bird smells in the woods.

We had nearly reached the end of the path when Corey suddenly stopped.

"Point!" he hissed.

We looked. Fifty feet ahead of us, on the edge of an old apple orchard, Cider was stretched out.

"There's the bird," whispered one of the other men, and then I saw it. The grouse was nonchalantly pecking fallen apples less than twenty feet in front of Cider.

We all stood there for a moment, staring at the tableau. The grouse bent down, jabbed at a frost-softened apple, straightened, high-stepped a few feet, bent again. Cider quivered but did not move.

"Bill, take him," said Corey.

I gripped my Savage with its one useless shotgun shell in the chamber. We didn't have enough time to argue about who should take the shot. I stepped forward and moved up behind Cider. He rolled back his eyes, as if to say, "About time somebody got here."

The bird was plainly visible on the ground in front of me.

"Shoot him," somebody said. "Just take him on the ground."

I remembered what Dad had told me on those occasions

when I'd shot a sitting grouse. "It takes a good hunter to get that close to a grouse. Nothing to be ashamed of."

"Quick," said one of the other men, "before he flushes."

I can't reconstruct all the thoughts that flashed through my mind. But I knew I had no desire to blast that grouse off the ground in full view of those four men. There was more shame in doing that, I believed, than in missing a fair shot at a flying bird.

Maybe it was all right for a kid, an apprentice grouse hunter, to shoot a grouse off the ground. It was not, I decided, all right for me.

So I stepped in front of Cider. The grouse craned his neck, then bent and scuttled forward. I took another step.

I didn't actually see the bird flush. I heard him, and with that explosion of wings my Savage came to my shoulder and swung on the bird as he rose in front of me. Some instinct beyond conscious thought aimed my shotgun and pulled its trigger for me.

The grouse fell. Cider pranced forward, picked up the stone-dead bird, and brought it to me. I knelt and accepted it from the dog's mouth. "Thank you," I said. I patted his muzzle. Then I stood, stroked the feathers of the grouse, and with careful nonchalance stuffed it into my game pocket.

The men didn't throw their hats into the air, or cheer, or pummel me with congratulations, for which I was grateful. For all they knew, I had shot plenty of flying grouse. "Nice shot," one of them said, and another said, "That was a pretty point, wasn't it?"

I glanced at Dad. He gave me a quick grin and a nod.

We hunted the rest of the Field and Stream cover but found no more birds. And during the long dark ride home to Massachusetts, Dad and I talked about the end of another hunting season, the men we'd hunted with, the days when we'd found our covers full of woodcock, and the days when they'd been empty. Dad allowed that we'd managed to end it on a positive note.

He didn't mention the fact that I had finally broken my streak. He said nothing about my decision not to shoot that grouse on the ground, or that I had decided well, or that he was proud of me.

He didn't need to.

———

I would like to report that after breaking my jinx I enjoyed a hot streak, or at least that I began to hit flying grouse with greater frequency. But it wouldn't be true. Oh, now and then I hit one. The law of averages did seem to operate, even in grouse hunting. But mostly I continued to miss. And I still do.

But it doesn't bother me at all anymore.

CHAPTER TEN

GONE FISHIN'

*I*n the natural course of things I grew up, graduated from college, and embarked on a career. I got married, and after a few years, when it became evident that the union was doomed, I called Dad. He was an old-fashioned man, and I wasn't sure how he'd respond. But I needed advice and understanding. It never occurred to me to seek it from anyone but Dad. "I need to talk to you," I said. "Just the two of us. Can you meet me?"

"Where and when?" were his only questions.

We met in a Howard Johnson's parking lot. We sat in the front seat of his car for several hours. I told him that he was right after all: Life sometimes could be stern and earnest.

"Don't blame yourself," he said, reading my mind, and for the first time he told me about his father's failed second marriage, his own harsh childhood, what a lucky man he was to have married my mother, and how raising a family is the most difficult and important thing a man has to do.

If a marriage is to be forever, he said, it ought to be a good one. Good marriages are rarer and more precious than good jobs.

I got custody of Bucky, my Brittany, and gave him up to his paternal grandfather for adoption.

When Dad and Mum retired to New Hampshire, I remained behind in eastern Massachusetts. I remarried, begat children, and did my best to follow Dad's example of devoting myself to their nurture. My kids and I walked the suburban woods and dangled worms for local bluegills. We took a few explores and expotitions.

I have never felt I have done as much or as well by my children as Dad did by me. His was a hard act to follow.

Aside from the forays with my kids, I didn't hunt and fish much during those years. When I did, it was mostly with Dad. Our excursions became ceremonial—a weekend of fly-casting for smallmouths on Winnipesaukee, an afternoon in the canoe on the Pine River or Beaver Brook, one October weekend a season in our old grouse and woodcock covers. These occasions had to be planned and plotted carefully. My life was filled with competing variables. We didn't have the leisure for spur-or-the-moment explores or elaborate expotitions. We fished and hunted when we could, which wasn't often, and where it was most convenient, which was in Dad's part of New Hampshire.

When Bucky died, Dad stopped hunting entirely. Grouse and woodcock hunting, he said, was no fun without a bird dog. I urged him to get another dog. No, he said, he had too many aches and pains to hunt anyway. Besides, it wouldn't be right to raise a dog who would outlive him. That was about fifteen years and two dog generations ago.

When I began to write, I quickly realized that one ought to write about what he knew and understood best. So I found myself reflecting on my times in the woods and on the water with Dad. In various actual and fictitious guises, he was usually the central character in my stories. And as I wrote about growing up a sportsman, I began to appreciate the central importance of the outdoors to my life. It was my legacy. More than anything else, it defined me. Dad had given me the outdoors, and I understood that I owed it to him to perpetuate it—not only by sharing it with my own children but also by writing about it and arguing for its preservation and by continuing to experience it myself.

So I began exploring the rivers than ran off the spine of the Continental Divide, and I found larger trout and more beautiful waters than I had imagined and land as nurturing to my soul as my New England. I hunted quail in Nash Buckingham country. I gained sporting companions of my own generation—Andy Gill, Keith Wegener, Elliot Schildkrout, Art Currier, Rick Boyer, Bill Rohrbacher, Cliff Hauptman, Blaine Moores, many others. And I wrote about these men and our adventures, and I showed my efforts to Dad. I gave him vicarious experience in exchange for his editorial red pencil.

As I was leaving Pond Road from a recent visit, Dad pointed to a cardboard box by the door. "Take that with you," he said. "I doubt if you'll find anything in there you can use, but help yourself."

The box, I knew, contained old books, and when I got home and took them out I found signed first editions by Harold Blaisdell, Ray Bergman, Corey Ford, John Alden Knight, Arthur MacDougall, Edmund Ware Smith, Burton Spiller, Ted Trueblood, Lee Wulff, and others. Most of the books had been inscribed "To Tap." They thanked him for his help on the manuscript, for his inspiration and support, for his friendship. They hinted at shared memories, partnerships cemented in canoes and woods, a common love and respect for the written word as well as for the outdoors.

They are leisurely books, most of them, books as devoted to adventure and fantasy and philosophy as practical lore, and I had devoured them as a boy. They were part of my outdoors legacy. They were treasure.

Most of these books, I realized with a kind of shock, had been written by men I had fished and hunted with who were no longer alive. They were men of Dad's generation, not mine. It was a generation that has nearly passed. Dad is among the few who are left.

It was a sobering realization.

But I smiled, too. "I doubt if you'll find anything in there you can use," Dad had said, as if an inscribed first edition by an old friend had value only insofar as it had utility. But that's always been his attitude toward what he scornfully calls *things*.

He has typed on the same clunky old Underwood for at least fifty years. "If it didn't work just fine" he says, and then shrugs, "I'd get another one."

My father is the least materialistic man I've ever known. He's not a collector. If anything, he's a divestor. He once owned dozens of bamboo fly rods, most of which had been given to him by their makers. He found the two or three that felt good and fished with them. The others gathered dust and became priceless classics. When fiberglass came along, Dad proclaimed it an improvement, and set about cleaning out his collection of the less-functional bamboo stuff. He gave those old rods to kids and casual acquaintances, anyone who expressed a mild interest in fishing. He never hesitated to help a potential fisherman get started, so he generally threw an old Hardy reel and a box full of Tap-tied flies into the bargain.

I suspect he gave away a lot of valuable stuff to shrewd bargain hunters who figured they knew a sucker when they saw one.

When I accuse him of naivete, he shrugs. "I don't give away anything I can use," he says. "What good is it if you can't use it?"

He swapped the pick of his bamboo fly-rod litter for a dry sink my mother coveted. When he needed new archery gear, he exchanged the classic old .410 double with which I shot my first pheasant for a cheap metal bow. When I expressed dismay, he seemed surprised. "I didn't think you'd want that old thing," he said. "You can't hunt anything with a .410. A most inefficient weapon."

"Yeah, well, I shot that pheasant with it."

"You shouldn't have been hunting pheasants with a .410 in the first place." Unassailable logic.

He has owned six guns in my lifetime (apparently gun manufacturers were not as generous with their samples as rodmakers): A Winchester Model 21 twenty-gauge double, which he bought in the 1930s and was the only gun he ever used for upland shooting; an Ithaca twelve-gauge pump, his duck gun; a lever-action .30-30 for deer; that .410 pheasant gun; a .22 revolver that he used for plinking rats at the town dump; and a single-shot .22 target rifle.

When he shot skeet, he owned a skeet gun. When he stopped shooting skeet, he got rid of that shotgun.

He had one gun for every purpose he could imagine. Each shot straight. He never needed any others.

The .410 is gone. The Winchester and the Ithaca stand now

in my gun cabinet. "I don't hunt anymore," said Dad when he gave them to me. "You might as well have them." He has kept the .30-30, although he tried to get me to take it. "You hang onto it," I said. "Just don't give it to a stranger." The .22 he keeps for woodchuck combat in his vegetable garden, although he doubts he will ever try to shoot the animals. "They're just doing what comes naturally," he says. "If they eat my lettuce, it's my fault for planting it there."

He gave the revolver to somebody, he doesn't remember who.

———

After many interstate telephone conversations, long-range weather analyses, medical reports, and consultations with Mum's tournament bridge schedule, we settle for a Thursday in June.

I leave Massachusetts early. Portal to portal, it's exactly ninety-eight miles, and it always takes precisely two hours. Every time I make the drive I tell myself that I should do it more often.

Usually I meet Dad and Mum half-way, at the Dunkin Donuts in Manchester. Dad and I exchange shopping bags containing magazines, paperback books, and random clippings that we think might interest the other. Mum generally slips a tin of brownies into the bag designated for me. We usurp a table, eat a donut, drink coffee, and talk. Sometimes I bring one of the kids along. We do this every two or three weeks.

But today we will fish, so I go the whole way.

We hoist Dad's little thirteen-foot Grumman atop his car and load our gear into the the back—a fly rod, a box of flies, sandwiches, canteen, two paddles, a push pole, the requisite floating cushions. Over the years we have weeded out the extraneous. Both of us like traveling light and spare.

The Pine River flows south to north from its origins in, of all places, Pine River Pond to its destination in Lake Ossipee. It's about fifteen miles long, and in its entire course it intersects just two passable roads, the second a major highway at its outlet. When Dad and I first fished it, we followed a network of dirt roads to an abandoned sandpit where we could leave the car close to the river's edge. But a few years ago somebody erected concrete posts and strung a padlocked chain across the entrance to the sandpit.

Now an iron bridge provides the only access to the Pine. We park and unload the car with the practiced efficiency of a partnership that is nearly half a century old. Then we confront the first decision of the day: Upstream or down? It's a question of minor importance. The water in either direction from the bridge is equally beautiful and navigable by canoe and inaccessible by foot. We expect beauty today, and we do not expect to see any other fishermen.

We will see many birds and animals. A moose would delight but not surprise us.

We do not expect to see any mayflies, and we do not expect to catch many trout. As with all of our fishing trips, we hope we will, but will not be disappointed if we don't. After all, we will have the river and each other's companionship, and those are enough for both of us.

We conduct our customary debate. Dad prevails and takes the stern. I am relegated to the bow. So I must fish, while he gets to paddle. On the Pine, the navigator generally accomplishes more than the fisherman. The paddler is always rewarded with the knowledge that he has done something both physical and skillful. I suspect that a man in his ninth decade especially relishes this affirmation, and I'm happy that Dad can experience it.

The Pine cuts through a mature forest, predominantly pine, oak, and maple. It's narrow and winding and studded with boulders. June-blooming wildflowers proliferate along its mud banks. In places we come to rocky riffles too shallow for the paddle, but Dad enjoys push-poling. It's a skill he has mastered, and he likes to practice it. Aside from the occasional riffle, the streambed is everywhere sand and silt — too sterile for significant aquatic insect life. A few times we have found fish rising to Red Quill hatches on the Pine, and then we have caught many trout. Those occasions were memorable. But we don't count on finding hatches or rising trout. We haven't hit a hatch in so many years that I wonder if they happen here at all anymore.

If the State of New Hampshire didn't stock the Pine with hatchery brook trout, it would be sterile of all fish life save chubs and yellow perch and pencil-size pickerel. They don't stock it heavily. We know the Pine will fill our limits of tranquility and companionship. Our expectations do not include trout.

Our Pine River routine is well fixed. We follow the river course slowly upstream under the canopy of overarching trees looking for a maverick rising trout. Eventually we will arrive at an impasse — a tree fallen across the river, riffles too shallow even to drag the canoe over. Then we will turn downstream. The fisherman will roll-cast a floating fly (the stream is too narrow and the bankside vegetation too thick for normal fly casting), twitching it against the banks and around the boulders. Since we rarely find rising trout, we catch most of our fish by teasing them up on the downstream leg.

I have brought one of my graphite fly rods today. Dad grumbles that his fiberglass rods do the job. I've been trying to convince him that what fiberglass was to bamboo, graphite now is to fiberglass. He remains stubbornly skeptical. I have tied on a little deerhair beetle, another decision that meets with his disapproval. We have always used yellow Cooper Bugs. They work fine.

We both believe that fly pattern makes no difference whatsoever on the Pine. Hatchery brookies here find no pellets, and not much of anything else, to eat. If they will take a weird yellow deerhair concoction like a Cooper Bug, they will take anything.

So I sit up in the bow, watching for birds and moose and mayflies and rising trout, and Dad paddles from the stern. Our conversation is unhurried and meandering, like our progress up the stream. The June sunlight filters through the trees, here and there dappling the water and spotlighting a clump of rioting wildflowers on the bank. Redwing blackbirds chitter in the bushes.

Nothing we see causes me to pick up my rod.

The river is low. At the first riffle I have to take off my shoes and socks and drag us through.

Just to clarify our purpose, I take a few random casts at likely trout hangouts, places where we have raised trout on past voyages.

I raise a chub and call it a trout.

Dad laughs.

We discuss writing and fishing, family and mutual friends. We tell each other stories that we both already know, playing our game of "Remember When?" We fill each other in on our separate lives, too.

At a party recently, I tell Dad, a woman accused me of being a "seething sadist" because I fished and hunted and glorified it in my writing. I felt defenseless under her assault. She forced me to admit that yes, my sport *did* sometimes — "Not that often," I impotently insisted — result in the death of what she called "innocent wild creatures." I told her that I did generally return the fish I caught. "Oh, sure," she said, "after you've had all your cruel pleasure from torturing and frightening the poor things."

"But, Jeez," I replied, "they're *fish!*"

"Sentient beings," she intoned, confident that she'd had the final word.

"I didn't know what to say," I tell Dad.

"You didn't have to say anything," he answers. "Hunting — and that includes fishing — is our heritage, our legacy. Our species has been doing it for something like three million years. Hunting required us to learn how to cooperate, divide labors, use tools, share — all the things you and I do when we're in the woods or on a river. These are good things. They make us human and they give us pleasure. You don't need to defend hunting or apologize for it. It's in our nature. It defines us." He smiles at me. "Hunting's in that woman's nature, too. She was hunting you."

A big pine, uprooted during a winter storm, has fallen across the stream to mark our upstream terminus. We haul the canoe onto the mud and carry our lunches up onto a sun-splashed spot on the bank. We remind each other to watch for rising trout while we eat.

Afterward we lie back on the grass. We listen to the music of the birds and the stream, and we gaze up through the laced tree branches to the sky, and it's easy to wind back thirty or forty years to other times when Dad and I have been together in the woods beside a stream. It never really mattered where we were or whether we had caught many trout or found a lot of birds. Time and place were irrelevant as long as we shared them.

Dad has been thinking the same thing. He says, "It's always good to get out, isn't it?"

"Yes," I say quietly. "It's always good."

Finally, as I have known he would, he stands up. "Don't want to let ourselves get all bogged-down and stiff-legged, now."

He wants to resume his seat in the stern.

"You like paddling and watching me fish?" I say.

"It's what I like the best."

"Well, me, too. You want to deprive me of that pleasure?"

He grins. "Sure."

But this time I prevail. We head downstream. Dad picks up my graphite rod, rolls out some line. Paddling and fly casting are two of his skills that have not rusted over the years.

"How do you like the rod?" I say.

"It's okay," he grumbles. "I don't see that it's any better than fiberglass."

He's trying to promote a debate. I smile at his back and decline.

He bites off the deerhair beetle and ties on a Cooper Bug. He probes the undercuts and boulders and runs, roll-casting the bug and twitching it back against the current.

We're nearly back to the iron bridge when something splashes at his fly. "Chub," I proclaim.

"Trout," he says.

He casts again. Another splash. He hooks it. "Chub," I re-peat.

"Trout."

He's right. He strips in, unhooks, and releases an eight-inch brookie.

"Good fishin', old timer," I say.

"Good guidin', young feller," he replies.